INTERDEPENDENCE OF FREE ENTERPRISE AND GOVERNMENTS IN THE GLOBAL MARKETPLACE

by
Raymond A. Robillard
University of Maryland

University Press
of America™

To My Wife

Jennie

TABLE OF CONTENTS

LIST OF TABLES

PREFACE

Today's market economy system has formed the basis for unparalleled economic growth throughout the world. Since World War II it also has brought a high level of prosperity for a relatively large number of people. The highest growth rates have been achieved, of course, by countries with liberal political-economic systems; mainly industrialized nations but including, as well, developing states such as Taiwan and South Korea. While other developing countries have participated in this growth in varying degrees close examination has shown that progress will of necessity continue to be relatively slow because of the need for long-range planning, intense technological training, huge capital investment and a new spirit, in those nations, of national and international political-economic cooperation.

Meanwhile the worldwide inflationary pressure of the energy crisis is temporarily confounding man's efforts to effect further improvement in the global economic arena. Nevertheless, exploration of the possibility of space colonization and industrialization is identifying a multitude of manufacturing, trade and development opportunities unsurpassed in the history of mankind.

This treatise, then, defends the need for free enterprise to assure economic growth. It reflects capitalism's ability to promote high standards and the free interplay between political power and economic decision making. The strengths and weaknesses of the system and the problems of free market behavior are identified and the conclusion is reached that capitalism will remain an important and viable factor in worldwide political economic structures and individual national development. Juanita Kreps, United States Secretary of Commerce, expressed this philosophy succinctly when she said "Commerce is the common language of the world's people, where ideologies divide, commerce unites."

ACKNOWLEDGEMENTS

My obligations are many in the development of this study. They include my indebtedness to Dr. Janos M. Bak of the University of British Columbia, Dr. Charles R. Foster, Executive Secretary of The Atlantic Council of the United States, Inc., Messrs. James R. Thrash and Keith R. Vail, Archivists at Maryland's Salisbury State College, and Dr. John R. Wennersten of the University of Maryland. These men, and Douglas Bergner, Researchist at the Johns Hopkins University School for Advanced International Studies, guided my research and subjected my writings to no end of constructive criticisms. To my wife Jennifer I owe a continuing obligation for her encouragement and for her perceptive observations on the draft of this work. I am indebted as well to Sharon Brodowski for careful and critical proofreading of the manuscript and its subsequent typing and finalization as a finished product.

I am grateful, too, to the friends who contributed so unselfishly of their advice and recommendations to the end of making the final manuscript a scholarly study worthy of its being.

Needless to say none of the individuals mentioned bear any responsibility for the views, or errors, which may be found in this work.

Raymond A. Robillard
Towson, Maryland

INTRODUCTION

Even though we live in an age of increasing global complexity, many people fail to perceive the relationship between politics and economics. Actually both disciplines are intimately connected in their marketplace orientation and have produced systems which accommodate many forms of enterprise and private ownership. Many of these enterprises are huge conglomerates which divorce ownership from personal involvement and have successfully contributed to national economic growth and to higher living standards within their sphere of influence. The foremost political economic system in the world today is capitalism which allows for decision making somewhat apart from political power and, thus, enables each to offset the other. In the chapters which follow United States free enterprise is examined in order to ascertain how it promotes growth and high living standards. The exact antithesis, Russia's rigid planned economy, is then reviewed in order to gain a perspective on the problems existing in an economy devoid of continuing entrepreneurial capital investment and producing no appreciable growth. The question is raised, therefore, whether free enterprise is essential for economic growth and whether some form of capitalism exists in all economies.

Since World War II Great Britain and the United States have subjected economic decision making in the private sector to increased governmental control. Bureaucratic inefficiency and needlessly stringent controls have resulted in a dramatic decline of England's economic growth with an accompanying loss of faith in that nation's currency by the international financial community. As private investment slowed, the government had to nationalize industry and inflate the money supply. Inflation set in at a seemingly exponential rate creating the illusion of prosperity. The labor unions, consequently, made ever-increasing annual wage demands which were met by the imposition of higher taxes on the middle classes. England's nationalization of industry has proven to be a dismal failure. In the

United States increased government control has
been exercised through the medium of regulatory
agencies. They are endowed with legislative,
administrative and judicial power and affect both
collective and individual endeavors. It has been
determined that there is a genuine need for regulation to prevent abusive and unscrupulous business practices. In recent years, however, the
regulated have tended to regulate the regulators.
Today's great political-economic need in the
United States appears, consequently, to be a re-
appraisal and reorganization of regulatory agencies and of the principles under which they operate. Yet, in view of the energy crunch which,
ostensibly, has produced a condition of pernicious inflation in the United States and throughout the world, it appears that corrective measures must include deregulation, development of
alternative energy supplies and the continued
pursuit of free trade.

During this period Japan is shown to have
wrought an economic miracle. This nation has indeed distinguished itself in industrial trade by
shifting its emphasis from the production of
labor-intensive products such as textiles, pottery and Christmas tree ornaments to steel,
ships, optical equipment, consumer electronics,
heavy machinery and sophisticated business machines. In order to accomplish this Japan has
developed a mixed economy patterned after the
American free enterprise system. The result has
been phenomenal growth, modernization of the
whole society without sacrifice of unifying traditions and an exceedingly viable industrial
economy competing successfully in the global marketplace.

In the Third World economic development has
proven to be a complex process subject to developing nations' many diverse responses to change.
Experience has shown that conventional economic
theory is largely irrelevant in coping with the
central problems of underdeveloped countries. It
appears, however, that these nations must develop
a well-balanced political-economic organization
in order to experience growth, gain a foothold in

the global marketplace and evolve a viable enterprise system in an international economic order.
Such a move has been undertaken by the People's
Republic of China which has taken a giant leap
into international trade.

It is not the task of this analysis to engage in theoretical model building. Rather, it
is the task of this paper to provide a perspective on economic decision making in the arena of
changing political options. Political economy,
that unique interaction of the market and the political process, remains neither immune to the
pressure of popular ideologies nor isolated from
cultural trends. Thus, this research has taken a
broad-based approach and has explored trends and
developments in economic decision making as seen
in both the literature of contemporary business
and current scholarship. Hopefully this study
will be of use to those seeking to understand the
complexities of economic growth within the general framework of national and international government regulations.

In this book capitalism's strengths and
weaknesses have been assessed and the conclusion
reached that the free enterprise system will not
vanish or collapse. It undoubtedly will not retain its present form but instead will be influenced by many political and economic factors.
Economist Milton Friedman, in his book "Capitalism And Freedom," long ago said, "I find it difficult to justify any alternative principle to
the capitalist ethic. The great achievement of
capitalism has been the opportunities it has of-
fered to men and women to extend and improve
their capacities."

CHAPTER I

THE FREE ENTERPRISE DOCTRINE

"Viewed as a means to the end of political freedom, economic arrangements are important because of their effect on the concentration or dispersion of power. The kind of economic organization that provides economic freedom directly, namely, competitive capitalism, also promotes political freedom because it separates economic power from political power and in this way enables the one to offset the other."

Milton Freidman, Economist
1976 Nobel Prize Winner

In the decades to come mankind's economic problems will be increasingly complex in detail and global in scope as nations escalate their struggle for access to markets and resources. This struggle will undoubtedly have a great impact on the political and social climate of many of the western nations, especially the United States. In that country the twin ideals of political and economic freedom have flourished during the past two centuries of leadership in the free enterprise economic system envisioned by its Founding Fathers. The degree of such freedom has, however, substantially altered with the passage of time. As little as forty years ago, the United States represented a form of economic and political society whose prospects and permanence were unquestioned. Robert Heilbroner, a distinguished economist, now speculates, however, that America currently "finds itself in a position of defensive insecurity and recognizes the presence of forces at work in the world whose impact on its destiny is neither wholly arbitrary nor wholly unpredictable."[1] If Heilbroner's position is sound then those who would seek to defend capitalism might do well to investigate the premises upon which the current economic order is based. A first step is to assess the strengths and weaknesses of the free enterprise doctrine in an era of rigid socio-economic change.

As early as the turn of the century Thorstein Veblen noted that

> "the economic welfare of the community at large is best served
> by a facile and uninterrupted interplay of the various processes
> which make up the industrial system
> at large; but the pecuniary interests of the businessmen, in which
> hands lies the discretion in the
> matter, are not necessarily best
> served by an unbroken maintenance
> of the industrial balance. It is,
> as a business proposition, a matter
> of indifference to the man of large
> affairs whether the disturbances
> which his transactions set up in
> the industrial system help or hinder
> the system at large, except insofar
> as he has ulterior strategic ends to
> serve."[2]

Taking Veblen's cue one can argue that, though the decisions of businessmen in their enterprises are perhaps more a matter of conscious calculation than are most human decisions, they are nevertheless motivated, not only by the hedonistic calculation of profit seeking, but as well by desires for power, prestige, social approval, creativity, playing the competitive game, independence, and by feelings of social obligations. According to sociologists Sylvia Koplad Selekman and Benjamin M. Selekman, "the ethics of business are not essentially different from those of a modern community; but that is because our whole civilization has generally adopted a set of ethical standards which are consistent with, and to some extent the historical result of, the requirements of business."[3] It is not surprising, therefore, that some of these standards weigh more with businessmen than with the rest of the community.

Veblen also observed that a good society

needs more than these virtues of the marketplace to assure that the freedom which is permitted one individual does not become a restraint on another. He stated that, "consequently, society needs working rules with which to regulate itself."[4] It needs mercy as well as justice, generosity as well as honesty, and mutual aid as well as self-reliance. A social environment and culture conducive to the expansion of business enterprise does not have to be one in which the ethical standards of business exclusively prevail; but at the same time, it must be one in which they are respected in word and fact. Deviations from such standards, brought to the attention of the courts by individuals and organizations, have determined over the years the meaning of property, liberty and value in the United States.

Property in a free enterprise economy has been identified as the ownership of things by individuals and, automatically has acquired the added attribute of power to withhold such things from the use of others; and this with the benefit of protections by statute. With the expansion of markets this power has taken on the characteristics of physical power, economic power and moral power all of which are exercised at one time or another through the interplay of free competition. Such a dynamic is the essence of liberalism a label which Joseph Schumpeter the famous London economist pointed out long ago "the enemies of the system of private enterprise have thought it wise to appropriate."[5] Capitalism's enemies maintain in fact that real liberalism exists only in a society where the means of production are owned and managed by the state and function "in conformity with the interests of the toilers."[6]

Liberal free enterprise doctrine depends upon individuals far more than the state. Liberalism, therefore, preaches self-sufficiency and the non-intervention of the state unless the voluntary efforts of the people fail. These efforts, according to economist Selig Perlman, include transactions involving "all legal tender and promises to pay, a man's calling, occupation,

trade, labor, the physical objects of his ownership, his right to choose an occupation or trade,
and the direction in which he would exercise his
labor."[7] The definition of labor, as used here
is intended to mean the individual's willingness
to use his faculties according to a purpose that
has been pointed out to him. He sells his promise to obey commands. He sells his goodwill.
From this point there has evolved the wage bargain which is carried out between the employer
and the employee predominantly through negotiations at the bargaining table by representatives
of industry and labor each acting on as collective a bargaining basis as possible.

    The modern corporations and the trade unions
today have great economic power which often enables them to contend on equal terms with the
modern state and with each other. The state
constantly strives in some respects, as Selig
Perlman sees it, "to regulate corporations and
the unions while they, in turn, each steadily
becoming more powerful, seek independence to the
highest degree possible."[8] Meanwhile, the corporations and the trade unions determine for individuals their rights, duties and liberties
within their own organization and in view of expected obedience to their own collective commands.

    It is apparent then that the most important
specific features of the free market economy are
the following: for the worker to choose his line
of work and his particular job; for the businessman, to choose his type of business, and set it
up at the place of his choice; for the investor,
to invest his capital in whatever enterprise he
chooses; finally, for the consumer, to buy the
product he prefers. We have noted too that an
additional essential characteristic of the capitalist economy is competition. This particular
feature is a direct result of the freedom of
trade and occupation, of contract, of property
and of profit-making.[9]

    The economic justification of competition
is that it keeps all the participants alert to

market changes and constantly on the lookout for
ways to increase efficiency and improve product
marketability. "By increasing his own efficiency," John R. Commons has written "the individual
worker or entrepreneur proportionately increases
the efficiency and production of the whole market."[10] This assertion assumes too that levels
of wages and prices remain fairly stable.

The sum and substance of free enterprise as
characterized here suggests that the market economy is the touchstone of all economic systems.
Prestigious economists have defined its dynamism and competitive process. Yet, while it has
many supporters in the global economy, no nation
has been as persistent a critic of capitalism as
the Soviet Union. Ironically, however, Russia
currently seems to have a burgeoning of non-
Marxist enterprise in its economic system.

FOOTNOTES

[1]Robert L. Heilbroner, The Future as History, (New York: Harper & Row, Publishers, 1959), 14.

[2]Thorstein Veblen, The Theory of Business Enterprise, (New York: The American Library of World Literature, Inc., 1958), 19.

[3]Sylvia Koplad Selekman and Benjamin M. Selekman, Power and Morality in a Business Society, (New York: McGraw-Hill Book Company, Inc., 1956), 29.

[4]Thorstein Veblen, The Theory of Business Enterprise, (New York: The American Library of World Literature, Inc., 1958), 20.

[5]Joseph Schumpeter, History of Economic Analysis, (New York: Oxford University Press, 1954), 394.

[6]William Ebenstein, Today's Isms, (Englewood Cliffs, New Jersey: Prentice-Hall, Inc., 1959), 121.

[7]Selig Perlman, A Theory of the Labor Movement, (New York: The Macmillan Company, 1928), 256.

[8]Ibid., 268.

[9]For excellent, more detailed discussion of this issue, see Ludwig von Mises, Planning for Freedom, (South Holland, Illinois: Libertarian Press, 1962), especially the chapter entitled "Wages, Unemployment and Inflation," and Henry Hazlitt, Economics in One Lesson, (New York: Harper and Brothers, 1946), especially the chapters entitled "Minimum Wage Laws" and "Do Unions Really Raise Wages?"

[10]John R. Commons, The Economics of Collective Action, (New York: The Macmillan Company, 1950), 106.

CHAPTER II

SOVIET CLOSET CAPITALISM

Just about ten years ago H. Akhminov, Soviet economist, observed that the socialist countries, especially the Soviet Union, are experiencing an ideological crisis. This distressing condition is reflected in their uncertainty as to the correct direction to take from the present stage of socialism to the fulfillment of the communist ideal.[1] In creating his economic model Marx maintained that both the means of production and the goods produced must remain in the hands of the state. He proclaimed, furthermore, that the business cycle was endemic and exclusive to capitalism. Over the years Marx's critics have pointed out that, nevertheless, he transferred all positive features of capitalism to communism, assuming that the leaders of the planned economy would be able to ascertain and regulate product demand and thus free the economy of the fluctuations that periodically plague the western world. In today's Soviet economy, which ostensibly emulates Marxist doctrine, an attempt is made to establish demand in that enterprise must submit to higher authority applications for goods they require, yet even orthodox Marxist economist Akhminov has noted that it is impossible to comply with such applications satisfactorily under a centralized system of economic management, with the result that demand loses its practical significance.[2] Consequently, in the Soviet Union the law of supply and demand does not operate. The economy is planned from the top and is proving to be as susceptible to cyclical vicissitudes as are other economies. Prices, arbitrarily fixed by the state, may play some role in statistics, but have no part in determining the real value of goods and do not reflect demand. Earlier, when everything was in short supply, the disadvantages of this system were not apparent, but with the start of mass production disproportions arose. Overproduction of some goods was accompanied by scarcity of others. The planners not only ignored the factories' applications for raw materials, but often ordered them to produce goods for which there was no demand.[3]

Soviet theorists have long realized that it would be possible to remove these obstacles if the economy were allowed to develop on market principles. To achieve this in an economy of the Soviet type, however, is more difficult than appears at first glance. This is evidenced by previous attempts to introduce elements of a market economy, as in 1948 for example, when Soviet planner N. Voznesensky tentatively pointed out the need for both monetary and cost accounting as a basis for long-range planning. He also protested the practice of allocating labor without any regard for costs.[4] In 1950, Voznesensky was shot for showing undue regard for planning and fiscal responsibility.

After Stalin's death, Voznesensky's fiscal precepts were revived. Political scientists Cocks, Daniels and Heer have pointed out that "problems of exact costing under market conditions and decentralization of industrial management became subjects for open discussion."[5] The most important feature of such debates, as written by well-known economist E. G. Liberman, was the suggestion that the criteria for the efficiency of any enterprise should be economic reform and profits. The importance of these factors lay in the need for centralized planning, genuine cost accounting, incentives for managers and increased directors' powers with regard to production scheduling. The real significance of these events was that they sparked free discussions of Soviet economic management, which in some cases even led to demands that "enterprises be denationalized and granted collective ownership of their capital."[6] Strumilin, another Soviet economist, claims that there are economists who wish to leave profits at the disposal of individual enterprises each of which would, as a leaseholder of state capital, acquire an inalienable right of ownership or claim to net profits. Other Soviet theorists (Rumyantsev, Khachaturov and Pashkov) speak in a joint article of certain economists who assert that, even under socialism, labor is a state commodity.

They observe that some are beginning to speak of controlled enterprise and even to regard it as a special form of commodity production. Soviet party leaders oppose this latter definition on ideological grounds. They feel that the consideration of market socialism as a form of commodity production is tantamount to saying that it is a variety of capitalism. They fear, too, that the regard of labor as a commodity which must be paid for according to its value would cause drastic changes in the entire wage structure and thus deprive the state of its advantage as a sole employer.[7] Moreover, Soviet leaders worry that the transformation of enterprises into leaseholders of state capital with the right to dispose independently of their profits would undermine the Party's monopoly of power.

Communist theorists are thus confronted with the unpleasant task of reconciling commodity production and socialism. Rumyantsev and his colleagues attempt to show that the mode of production is determined by property relations rather than by production. They claim that under socialism the money-commodity relationship and the law are very different from their capitalism counterparts.[8] These sentiments contradict the Marx-Lenin thesis that egalitarian utilization of land is not a socialist precept; rather, that their doctrine calls for the abolition of private property. While the advocates of further economic reforms call for the introduction of fuller economic accountability, Rumyantsev and his associates speak disapprovingly of economists who appear to believe that fiscal responsibility serves under socialism as the main regulator in the growth of the entire economy. These diverse views among Soviet economists are only a reflection of the deep conflict between the Party apparatus and the technical intelligentsia on the issue of who, the Party leaders or the people in charge of production, should dispose of profits. Thus, Soviet ideologists, while resorting to complex solutions, are now having to present certain capitalistic phenomena as essential prerequisites for the development of socialism. It would, of course, be

incorrect to deduce from this ideological con-
fusion that a political crisis is brewing. It
does, however, indicate that, as G. E. Schroeder,
a noted economist, pointed out "Communism has
passed the peak of its development as a political
doctrine and is entering the stage of reaction."[9]
This is evidenced by the Soviet Union's own calculations of 1976 growth rates as the lowest in
over twenty five years.

In fact many Westerners predict that the
main goals of the current efficiency and quality
five-year plan, which runs through 1983, will
not be met. Soviet leaders claim that the self-
less work of the people will yield remarkable
new results. Western economists retort that the
country still hasn't begun to solve its efficiency problem. Their thinking is based on the
conviction that labor shortages resulting from
a declining Russian birth rate will help force
the economy down from four percent to approximately three percent in the next year or two.
They note, furthermore, that production is far
below target. This includes the output of oil,
electricity and natural gas which will no doubt
intensify the Soviet energy crunch. Despite
the economic disappointments there is pressure
from the nation's leadership and from the people
for an increase in food and consumer goods production.[10]

Whether the men who run the Soviet Union
will, as a result, loosen their control of the
economy enough to make proposed reforms succeed
is doubtful. Throughout Soviet discussion of
economic reform, as Time magazine pointed out
several years ago, runs an unstinted but central
theme:

> "liberalization of the economy
> might lead to political heresy.
> In the view of some western ex-
> perts, the combination of econo-
> mic reform and disintegration of
> Communist Party control in Czecho-
> slovakia in 1968 weighs on the
> minds of Soviet leaders as they

consider how far to go with
reforms at home."11

Despite its seemingly rigid orthodoxy the
Soviet Union is setting up profit-minded corporations in the West. The Russians have undertaken investments in shipping, banking, insurance and even computers. Russian business be-
haves much like American and European conglomerates that look abroad to further their commercial interests. Indeed, the Soviet Union has
gone multinational. It operates a network of
banks in Western Europe, the Mideast and Asia.
It owns insurance companies and equipment-
leasing firms in several Common Market countries.
It has formed some thirteen maritime agencies
around the world two of which are located in
the United States. These agencies are charged
with the task of locating customers for Soviet-
owned transworld shipping lines. The U.S.S.R.
owns and manages more than a score of companies
in the capitalist world to sell raw materials,
such as oil and lumber, or to sell and service
its manufactured products, such as tractors and
automobiles.12

All these companies are incorporated in the
countries where they operate and issue whatever
documents and statistics that are required by
local laws. Even their annual reports are, in
most cases, the sort of glossy, handsomely prin-
ted booklets one would expect from multibillion $
capitalist corporations. Some even include a
letter to shareholders from their chairman of
the board crediting success to skillful management and blaming setbacks on adverse business
conditions.13

As western economists have recognized "to
an impressive degree Soviet-owned companies in
the capitalist world are staffed by non-Russian
executives who are citizens of the host countries."14 Some of the Soviet Union's western-
based businesses earn high profits. Others do
not fare very well and some even lose money.
Many of them are not required by host country
law to disclose their earnings. And, like any

13

western home office, Moscow is highly selective
about the financial information it volunteers.
Soviet leaders, according to Andrei Sakharov,
the dissident physicist and Nobel laureate,
appear to have recognized, belatedly, that the
chances for eventual economic prosperity, and
perhaps even for survival, depend upon developing a permanent market relationship with the rest
of the industrialized world. They recognize,
however, that the Soviet Union faces a technology gap with the industrialized West that puts
the U.S.S.R. into a "different age."[15] It would
be difficult, therefore, to increase exports of
raw materials because the Soviet Union needs
massive amounts of expensive western technology
in order to extract more of those resources.
For example, the Russians do not have the machinery they need to develop their vast oil and
natural gas reserves the production of which is
not increasing as fast as planned or hoped. According to America's Central Intelligence Agency
forecasts reserves are proving technologically
more and more difficult and expensive to exploit
to the degree that over the next decade the
Soviet Union will change from a net exporter to
a substantial importer of oil.[16]

Thus, only by importing the required technology can the Russians increase exports. Yet,
without increasing them, they cannot afford the
imports they want and need. According to E. G.
Liberman "even if they manage to develop their
own machinery for recovering additional quantities of oil and other raw materials, their ability to export these materials for hard currency
will be severely limited."[17] The Soviet Union's
own need for natural resources is expanding
sharply. Domestic oil consumption, for example,
has more than doubled during the last ten years
and is expected to double again by 1990. Furthermore, the quantity of raw materials needed
by the Eastern European satellites has also
been expanding sharply. "For political reasons,"
Liberman adds, "the Russians prefer to continue
serving as chief supplier to their satellites,
rather than make use of those raw materials
for expansion of exports to the West."[18] Be-

TABLE 1

COMPONENTS OF U.S. - SOVIET TRADE
(in Billions of dollars)

YEAR	Soviet Export to U.S.	Other U.S. Exports	U.S. Agricultural Exports	Total Trade	Soviet Debt To The West
1970	.10	.15	.00	.25	1.9
1971	.09	.21	.00	.30	2.8
1972	.10	.16	.39	.65	3.5
1973	.20	.30	.90	1.40	3.7
1974	.30	.35	.35	1.00	4.5
1975	.25	.70	1.05	2.00	10.7
1976	.24	.81	1.45	2.50	16.0
1977	.26	.50	1.24	2.00	19.0

SOURCE: FORTUNE Research, FORTUNE, Volume 97, January 16, 1978, Herbert E. Meyer "Why The Outlook Is So Bearish for U.S.-Soviet Trade."

NOTE: Grain sales have been the major elements of United States-Soviet trade. To stimulate continued economic growth, the Russians have spent billions of dollars on joint industrial projects. Their huge indebtedness to the capitalist world, generated by imports of equipment, technology and food, has created a need for the Soviets to cut back spending.

cause of this powerful combination of reasons
and circumstances Soviet leaders hope to trans-
form the U.S.S.R. from an irregular exporter of
raw materials to an established exporter of manufactured products on a scale large enough to satisfy the country's need for hard currency to
pay for Western imports. A reversal of the
West's economic success added to an increase in
exports and the curbing of western imports would
help the Kremlin immeasurably in its efforts to
keep the growing external debt in bounds. A
concrete move to control the balance of payments
deficit is the current effecting of barter deals
where suppliers agree to accept one hundred percent payment in the form of counter-deliveries.
Berthold Beiz, Chairman of West Germany's Krupp
Industries, says that "East-West trade is starting to become like the barter trade of the
Stone Age: wooden clubs in exchange for bone
tools, bones for pelts, and pelts as payment for
flint axes."[19] Establishing profit-minded companies in the capitalist world appears to be
still another means for the Soviet Union to par-
ticipate in World trade. The rules and inner
workings of such trade presently are a mystery
to most Soviet officials; however they are
learning. What remains to be seen is whether the
Russians are really prepared for the political
costs of interdependence and for effecting the
internal political and economic changes that a
permanent, large-scale trading relationship
with the capitalist countries will require of
them.[20]

By working diligently to learn the complexities of doing business in the West, the financial technicalities and the demand of customers
for good products and good servicing, the Russians may well succeed in developing a market
for their manufactured goods, along with a cadre
of business executives capable of selling them.
These executives, however, may be defeated by
the complications and contradictions in the
western economic system. Since the Soviet economy is centrally planned in rigid five-year segments it appears that factory production schedules are not easily adjusted to absorb the mar-

ket vagaries of unpredicted sales of basic products nor of related parts.

Time and again Soviet leaders have refused
to allow the law of supply and demand, rather
than planning, to set production schedules and
prices. This often leaves the country's economy
out of phase with the unplanned, hugely volatile
economies of the capitalist world. Some kind of
a link is needed if the U.S.S.R.is to succeed as
an exporter of manufactured goods to the West on
a regular basis.

The Russians are currently trying to strat-
egize their way around the problem. In February
1976, in a speech to the twenty fifth Party Congress, Premier Alexei Kosygin suggested that the
U.S.S.R.develop what he called an export sector.
As Kosygin described it, this sector would be
roughly analogous to the Soviet Union's defense
sector. That is, it would be a thing apart from
the rest of the economy. It would get top priority for money and managerial talent, and it
would be geared to meet higher standards of productivity and quality than, for example, the consumer products sector. Kosygin even proposed
that factories be built solely to manufacture
goods for export to the West. Lending support to
Premier Kosygin's recommendations in a December
1977 speech to the Supreme Soviet, Nicolai K.
Baibakov, the nation's planning chief, criticized
past economic performance in the volume of United
States-Soviet trade. In a related speech Nikolai
Inozemtsev, Director of Russia's Institute of
World Economy and International Relations in
Moscow, asserted that "we are going to export oil
in the mid-80's and we are going to export in
rather substantial quantities."21

It seems doubtful, however, that an export
sector as visualized by Premier Kosygin could be
workable. For one thing, Soviet planners may
prove unwilling to allocate the required financial and human resources. Certainly the creation of a new top priority sector will be opposed somewhat forcibly by powerful officials in
the defense sector. Moreover, if an export sec-

tor were actually maintained as a thing apart,
the Soviet goal of improving productivity
throughout the economy by absorbing western
equipment and technology would be thwarted.
Finally, by its very nature, an export sector
would be linked to the economic and political
world beyond the Soviet Union's closely guarded
borders.

The increased numbers of executives and
managers who would be assigned to it would of
necessity spend long periods of time living and
working in the West exactly as a carefully selected few do now. They would negotiate with
western business men, socialize with them, dress
like them and, inevitably some would begin to
think like them. "The possibility of ideological infection from extended exposure to the Free
World," writes Fortune editor Herbert E. Meyer,
"terrorizes Soviet leaders to the degree that
they appear still to be unwilling to risk the
political hazards of the global marketplace."[22]

There is good cause for such concern. In
Russia underground trade has become a way of
life. It is systematic and includes a large
variety of consumer goods. Practically any
material or service can be obtained. As a
matter of fact Izvestia disclosed on January 1,
1975 that more than one-third of the country's
private motorists were driving on stolen state-
owned gasoline. Since then the black market has
grown beyond control and there are now, as well,
various shades of gray market in which Russians
openly offer fistfuls of rubles for just about
any kind of Western merchandise. It doesn't
stop there however. Representatives of Western
companies doing business in the Soviet Union
have discovered entire underground industries.
They have found, furthermore, that on occasion
bribes of three to five percent of gross contracts and other business sweeteners as well are
expected and volunteered. It has become clear
that Russian creeping capitalism has expanded.
Inflation is rampant. And, all of this is a
direct result of the economy's inefficiencies,
shortages, poor quality goods and terrible de-

lays in service.[23]

This, then, is the problem of Marxist enterprise without benefit of an export market and without a legalized private trade sector. The economic results for the Socialist Soviet Union can hardly compare with those of successful laissez-faire capitalism in the United States. Both systems have thus far provided an insight, each from its own philosophical base, on the dynamics of political-economic organization. Diverse economic systems must be studied, however, to understand the effect of controls and regulations imposed on laissez-faire enterprise. Great Britain is, therefore, an interesting study in the problems of a socialist mixed economy where industrial nationalization is at the forefront of all economic activity.

FOOTNOTES

1. H. Akhminov, "Market Socialism Embarasses Soviet Ideologists," Institute for the Study of the USSR Bulletin, June 1968, 10.

2. William Baumol, "Smith v. Marx on Business Morality and the Social Interest," "The American Economist, Fall 1976, 41.

3. H. Landreth, "Creeping Capitalism in the Soviet Union?" Harvard Business Review, September 1967, 134. Additionally, refer to Gertrude Schroeder, "Recent Developments in Soviet Planning and Incentives," Soviet Economic Prospects for the Seventies, Joint Economic Committee, (Washington: GPO, 1973), 36. Also see Paul Gregory and Robert Stuart, Soviet Economic Structure and Performance, (New York: Harper & Row, 1974), chapter 10.

4. G. E. Schroeder, "Soviet Economic Reforms: A Study in Contradictions," Soviet Studies, July 1968, 5.

5. Paul Cocks, Robert V. Daniels and Nancy Whittier Heer, The Dynamics of Soviet Politics, (Cambridge: Harvard University Press, 1977), 331.

6. R. N. Carew Hunt, The Theory and Practice of Communism, (Harmondsworth, England: Penguin Books, Ltd., 1963), 271. For further investigation refer to Abram Bergson, "Soviet Economic Perspectives: Toward a new Growth Model," Problems of Communism, March-April 1973, 1-9.

7. H. Akhminov, "Market Socialism Embarasses Soviet Ideologists," Institute for the Study of the USSR Bulletin, June 1968, 20.

8. "Russia's Trouble With Reforms," Time, January 26, 1970, 72.

9. G. E. Schroeder, "Soviet Economic Reforms: A Study in Contradictions," Soviet Studies, July 1968, 1.

10. Eric Morgenthaler, "Comrades Wanted: Soviet Needs Workers; Shortage Poses Threat To Economic Growth," Wall Street Journal, August 17, 1978, 1-26.

11. "Russia's Trouble With Reforms," Time, January 26, 1970, 72.

12. Russia's overseas corporations are wholly owned by the USSR through various ministries, agencies and larger Soviet companies or are owned jointly with non-Soviet businesses. Note Joseph Berlinger's The Innovation Decision in Soviet Industry, Cambridge: MIT Press, 1976).

13. Franklyn Holzman, International Trade Under Communism, (New York: Basic Books, 1976), 138.

14. Ibid., 141.

15. John Dornberg, "Recession Communist Style," Dun's Review, April 1977, 84.

16. Soviets Say They'll Have Oil To Export," The Wall Street Journal (Global Report), May 8, 1978, 6.

17. E. G. Liberman, "Role of Profits in the Industrial Incentive System of the USSR," International Labor Review, January 1968, 2.

18. Ibid., 3.

19. "Big Slump in East-West Trade," Dun's Review, April 1978, 121.

20. Franklyn Holzman, International Trade Under Communism, (New York: Basic Books, 1976), 168-169.

21. "Soviets Say They'll Have Oil To Export," The Wall Street Journal (Global Report), May 8, 1978, 6.

22. Herbert E. Meyer, "This Communist International Has A Capitalist Accent," FORTUNE, February 1977, 148.

23. "SSSSST! Wanna Sell Your Levi's?" Dun's Review, November 1978, 110. The subject of corruption in the Soviet Union is broadly covered in Chapter III of The Russians by Hedrick Smith (New York: Ballantine Books, 1976).

CHAPTER III

THE BRITISH EXPERIENCE:
PROBLEMS OF NATIONALIZATION

Though Great Britain is very much involved in the global struggle for markets and resources it is equally, if not more, concerned over the state of its own political-economic organization. In fact, the government's economic problems are so acute that the British have rejected industrial nationalization as their alternative to capitalism. Its post-World War II economic experience with the nationalized industries is of sufficient magnitude and longevity as to make possible an overview of both the system and its problems in a proper free enterprise perspective. Nationalization in the United Kingdom covers both the public utilities and the private industry sectors of the economy. We will use as a model for our investigation, however, only the nationally-owned productive enterprises such as coal, iron, steel, transport, etc. These are excellent examples of the process which makes of the British economy a mixed economic system.

The term mixed economy came into general use after World War II. It is a simple concept based on the assumption that the national economy is composed of two distinct parts. They are the private sector, i.e., industry and commerce dominated by market influences, subject to the laws of competition and working for profit and the public sector which is represented by central and local government and organized to provide services which do not operate for profit and which are not subject to competition.[1] These sectors are clearly defined in Britain's first White Paper on Employment Policy which in May 1944 laid down Keynesian guidelines for post-World War II national economy policy. This document was the effort of a coalition government and represented a consensus between the Conservatives and the Laborites. It further defined public utilities as "statutory monopolies under which the state, in return for the grant of a monopoly, laid down strict conditions for their operation and for setting rates charged to consumers for their services."[2]

It is interesting to note that the government avoided control of public utilities capital programs. They felt that more power of direction was needed to control substantial acceleration of investments in new capital expenditures. In the area of private enterprise, however, a general stabilization policy was initiated to supplement government monetary policy. Its purpose was to encourage the private sector to plan its own capital expenditures in conformity with government regulations.

Since the White Paper on Employment Policy appeared all British governments, regardless of their party identity, have put full employment in the forefront of all their policy planning. This is because the high unemployment of the inter-war years bit deeply into the consciousness of the nation which decided that such a tragedy must never recur. They were reinforced in this view by Keynes' 1936 publication of the General Theory of Employment, Interest and Money which provided a basis of economic theory and principles on which to work out and maintain a policy of full employment. In this book Keynes made it clear that "the central controls necessary to ensure full employment would, of course, involve a large extension of the traditional functions of government."[3]

Such a great increase in government control naturally aroused doubts in Keynes' mind. While noting that the authoritarian State system seems to solve the problem of unemployment at the expense of efficiency and freedom, he went on to say that

> "it is certain that the world will
> not much longer tolerate the un-
> employment which is associated
> with present-day capitalistic in-
> dividualism. It may be possible
> by a right analysis of the problem
> to cure the disease while preser-
> ving efficiency and freedom."[4]

Keynes' work appeared at a critical time. As he himself said "at the present moment, people are usually expectant of a more fundamental diagnosis; more particularly ready to receive it; eager to try it out, if it should be even plausible." Between the appearance of his book and the White Paper were eight years of economic depression and high unemployment during which government and its advisors absorbed Keynes' doctrine. It expressed the principle that the government accept as one of its primary aims and responsiblities the maintenance of a high and stable level of employment after the war. Keynes added that the government believed widespread unemployment could be prevented by a policy of maintaining total internal expenditure if necessary expansion of external trade could be assured. This last statement has dogged Britain since the war, with its problems of exports, balance of payments, inflation of currency and devaluation. Keynes rather optimistically assumed that

> "if nations can learn to provide
> themselves with full employment
> by their domestic policy, there
> need be no important economic
> forces calculated to set the in-
> terest of one country against that
> of its neighbors and that there
> would be a willing and unimpeded
> exchange of goods and services in
> conditions of mutual advantage."[5]

During the Attlee government, Britain nationalized coal, gas, electricity, railways, road transport and steel. This was the remedy for an industrial economy that was in shambles after six years of war. The economy was almost literally bankrupt. Added to Britain's woes was the traumatic experience of dismantling the Empire. In fact Britain, in 1947, decided to give up India, the Pearl of the Empire. Apart from industrial nationalization there were controls surviving from the war which were considered by many Socialists as providing a fabric for a Socialist economy.

> "But many of these were soon out

> of date and became ridiculous;
> what is the use of a system of
> licensing designed for scarcity
> in wartime when the rapid post-
> war expansion produced a super
> abundance of licensed goods?
> So there was a bonfire of con-
> trols in which Mr. Harold Wilson
> gloried when President of the
> Board of Trade and which still
> existed when the Labor government
> departed in October 1951. They
> were almost entirely swept away
> by the Churchill government in
> the next few years."6

It is a common belief that the Attlee government was collectivist and set the country on
the road to collectivism. If anything it is the
reverse of what happened. The nationalization
measures were, in spite of strong class antag-
onisms, the fulfillment of a long-range plan
going back a generation. Apart from the public
utilities, the campaign was concerned with industries which had been predominant in the nine-
teenth century and which, it would develop, were
to play a lesser role in the second half of the
twentieth century.

Now what effect had these developments on
the relations between the government and the private sector? Though the government was, during
the nineteen fifties, making financial and economic decisions in the national interest when it
concerned the public sector, these decisions
were still clearly detached from the private
sector. It is, of course, true that

> "in the post-war period the pri-
> vate sector had to keep a more
> careful watch on government
> policy than before the war. For
> one thing, the burden of taxation
> was so heavy that changes in taxa-
> tion had serious effects. This
> was particularly true with purchase
> tax which, levied on the products
> of the modern industries such as

motor cars, domestic appliances
and electronic goods, could have
very unsettling effects."[7]

Changes in purchase tax and hire purchase
conditions were repeatedly used to boost or de-
press consumption; but, as W. A. Robson noted,
"governments were not yet treating the public
and private sectors alike in their attempts to
evolve a macro-economic policy."[8]

There was, however, one respect in which
the presence of a public sector was beginning to
have effects on the private sector. The long
campaign to bring about nationalization was
based on the Fabian Society's belief that the
worker would benefit when the private employer
and his profit disappeared and, thus, there
would be more for the workers. This and other
socialist doctrines have been advanced since
1884 when the society was founded by prestigious
writers and wealthy idealists. Early members included George Bernard Shaw, Sidney and Beatrice
Webb, H. G. Wells, and Graham Wallas. These
thinkers and their followers were responsible
for the awakening of the working class.[9] The
workers in the nationalized industries, therefore, regarded it as natural that they should
have first claim on the proceeds of the industry
in which they worked. If that industry was in a
strong monopoly position, such as coal was up to
1958, it was expected that the employees would
receive regular increases. In the case of the
miners this policy would put them in the forefront as the best paid workers. As a matter of
fact the annual reports of the British Coal
Board show that, from 1947 to 1957 the miners had
attained strong bargaining position. The output
of coal was never enough. On the whole the
nation had a guilty conscience about the suffer-
ings of the miners in the inter-war years and
most people believed, consequently, that the position of the miners was justified considering
the hazards of their work and their poor rewards
before the war. Demand for coal was inelastic
and frequent price increases did not seem to
check the demand. Thus between 1947 and 1957

wages about doubled and in line with this went
the cost of raising a ton of deep-mined coal and
the price obtained for it. Between 1957 and
1967 increases in price became infrequent.
There was no general increase between September
1960 and April 1966. It was only the 50 percent
increase in productivity between 1957 and 1967
which enabled miners to secure increased earnings. But otherwise their bargaining position
was weak. With huge stocks of coal lying un-
sold on the ground a strike would have been futile and the miners and their leaders were aware
of the change in their strength and practiced
restraint. Between 1957 and April 1968 manpower
in the industry declined from 710,000 to 361,
000. This tremendous decline meant that the
Coal Board had to meet reasonable demands for
increased pay and improved conditions; otherwise
the rundown of the industry would have accelera-
ted disastrously.

But even in an industry such as railways,
which had no monopoly strength and was obviously
declining, the workers' claims for improved pay
and conditions could not be resisted. As early
as 1951, Aneurin Bevan, as Minister of Labor,
had pressured the Transport Commission to improve an offer to the railwaymen. Hardly a
year passed in the fifties without increases
being secured and Ministers, including the Prime
Minister, would intervene. In 1960 the Guillebaud Committee laid down the principle that
railwaymen should have their wages determined on
a specific comparison with the pay of workers in
other industries; the principle was accepted by
all concerned. A substantial pay raise was immediately awarded and followed annually by further increases.[10]

The railways did not have the money to pay
the higher wages. In the fifties Ministers occasionally warned the Transport Commission that
they would not put up the money required, but
all to no effect. The increases became the
source of the money, not the customers. The
trade unions quickly sensed the importance of
these developments. They recognized that, if

the nationalized industries were compelled to provide increases from the bottomless pocket of the taxpayer through annual rounds of wage claims, workers in the private sector would follow suit. Hence, since the late fifties production costs in the nationalized industries have adversely affected operating costs in the private sector. As a result product prices increased rapidly causing frequently expressed consumer complaints.

When the nationalized industries could no longer generate sufficient profits to finance their own development, the necessary funds had to be provided by loan from the government. In turn the government raised funds by keeping taxation at the necessary level. In 1961 another White Paper, entitled "Government Expenditures Below The Line," was published to define lending parameters. This was followed in 1968 by the establishment of the National Loans Fund and the titling of this annual White Paper was changed to "Loans From The National Loans Fund." Financing of this new fund came from built-in budget surpluses thus causing the development of the nationalized industries to be made possible by continually heavier taxation of the private sector.[11]

Now that the government had developed the habit and techniques for influencing and even controlling the policies of the nationalized industries, economic problems increasingly beset the government and it was only natural for it to extend the influence acquired over the public sector. Invaluable lessons had been learned in dealing with the public sector. The government in the fifties and sixties was forced to adopt various kinds of controls in order to guide and regulate the national economy in the manner desired by the government. These controls, to be effective, must affect both private and public sectors. Many of them are not obvious to the public; Boards and Ministers agree on a policy which has usually been announced as a Board's decision. But the pattern is changing and it has been generally admitted in recent years that open decisions have been taken by the government. It is becoming more and more difficult for the Boards to make a decision of importance without consulting the government. The private sector, therefore, despite the government's commitment to it, "has been harmfully influenced by nationalization. The government failed to recognize the interrelationship of the two sectors and ended up treating both badly."[12]

So the stage was set for serious changes for the private sector in the sixties and seventies. Fifteen years after the end of the war the strains and stresses of post-war economic policy, or lack of policy, were becoming grimly apparent. Britain pursued all the desirable features of life simultaneously; or tried to. "The people demanded a welfare state with ample social services, which necessitated high taxation."[13] Full employment was insisted on; even a small number of unemployed was regarded as objectionable. The newly assumed role of the state in managing the national economy led to the general belief that the state was able to help people with all their problems. The equipment of the state for managing the national economy had not, however, been adequately developed, for

> "the machine of government hung
> uneasily suspended between the
> pre-war laissez-faire attitude
> and the post-war philosophy of
> control and management; but, as
> ever, Ministers were moved by
> short-term considerations and
> adjustments and so Britain slid
> into a number of stop-go crises."[14]

The great burden of the British Empire was the fundamental need of the British economy for an export market. This issue did not receive the deep consideration to which it was entitled even though all plans for a healthy mixed economy after the war depended on a flourishing, thrusting and highly competitive export trade. Yet, Mr. Macmillan found the task of explaining the need for exports difficult since the climate of public opinion was indifferent to the subject.

The nationalized industries sold their products in the home market and the private sector manufacturers who did produce goods for export had to buy the raw material products of these industries at ever rising prices. Meanwhile the government was not finding solutions. It recognized that some economic good had to be sacrificed to achieve, and inevitably the sacrifice was the value of the pound which, through steady inflation, fell by over forty percent between 1946 and 1960. Relief was, of course, given by the devaluation of the pound in 1949; but by 1960 the exchange value of the pound was becoming badly out of line with its depreciated value internally. The result was the stop-go crises of the fifties.

Meanwhile the Labor Party had launched in 1957 plans for supervising the five hundred twelve large units in the private sector. These companies were defined as those with assets exceeding two and a half million pounds. It was suggested that in these organizations the shareholders are functionless and the managements, therefore, are in control and exercise enormous power without being responsible to anybody.

> "The essential point is that the Boards of these companies should conduct their affairs in a manner which coincides with the interests of the community. This involves not only good relations with their employees and full consideration of the consumer interests, but also a sense of responsibility to the nation as a whole, through Parliament and the government. These might well be the terms of a nationalization act. Seven years after this document, Labor took office. At first it had a tiny majority of four; but after March 1966 it had a handsome majority."[15]

Throughout its six years of office, the Labor government was harassed by an infinitude of

financial and economic problems, especially in
connection with the balance of payments. This
condition, including rebudgeting every few
months and constant course changes, lasted well
into the 1960's and precluded embarking on long-
term policies. Nevertheless an attempt was made
through the Industrial Reorganization Corporation created in January 1966. This organization
was brought under the aegis of the Department of
Economic Affairs and was independently empowered
to draw up to one hundred fifty million pounds
for its projects. Its charter provided for the
promotion of industrial efficiency and profita-
bility in order to improve the economy. It was
authorized to promote or assist the reorganization or development of any industry and to establish and promote or assist in the establishment and promotion of new industrial enterprises.
The corporation functioned until 1970 when it
was abolished by the Conservative government.
During the four years of its existence the Industrial Reorganization Corporation's staff concentrated its efforts on mergers and reorganiza-
tions always seeking to implement benefits to
the balance of payments and avoiding loss of
control to foreign interests.[16] The activities
of the corporation were largely directed to the
more modern industries such as electrical manufacturing, electronics, motor cars and ball
bearings. Another main instrument for controlling industry was the National Board of Prices
and Incomes which functioned from 1965 to 1970.
There was some overlap with the Monopolies Commission which was also trying to control monopoly profits. The investigations of the National Board for Prices and Incomes constituted government intervention in industry aimed at increasing efficiency and production. From 1967
the Board was given responsibility for investi-
gating all applications by the nationalized industries for price increases.[17]

In 1968 government powers were further extended by passage of the Industrial Expansion
Act. The government was now empowered to give
loans, grants and guarantees for various general purposes such as improving efficiency or pro-

ductivity or developing technological improvements; the last was a favorite theme of the Prime Minister. The main uses made of the powers under the Act were in the field of computers and aluminum smelters. Finally there was substantial help for the shipbuilding industry. This started off with grants for modernization made under the Shipbuilding and Industry Act of 1967 but went on to become a series of subsidies.

The Labor government was thus intervening actively over a wide range of industries. The original proposals in 1957 had become a series of ad hoc measures prompted by repeated crises. The economy was becoming very mixed; the borderline between the public and private industrial sector was becoming blurred. Government control over the former was stronger and more continuous than over the latter simply because it had become systematic and had been operating for some years. Intervention in the private sector was not backed by adequate government machinery for supervision and follow-through; a defect which had been apparent in government relations with the nationalized industries, but where twenty years had brought some improvements. Though the presence of the public industrial sector was a temptation to the Labor government to widen the sphere of its influence and control over all industry, it appeared too harassed by pressing problems such as balance of payments to devise adequate and considered methods of extending that control. So the result was a series of makeshifts, the results of which included a failure to appreciate the complexities of this sort of intervention and to be over-optimistic about the size and speed of its effects. Furthermore, when the business community became disillusioned, all the difficulties and differing views of what policy should be, the hostility of intervention, the role of the Civil Service and the constant interaction between these worsened.

Significantly, economist Andrew Graham, British Parliamentary documentarian, wrote that "the apparent failure and inconsistencies which emerged were much more a function of the constraints within which policies were expected to work than an indication of a failure of the policies themselves."[18] Yet, all governments are plagued with constraints and such policies of intervention should not be treated as isolated philosophical concepts which can be applied to a world free from human troubles and passions.

By June 1970 steel had been renationalized and a bill to nationalize all ports was introduced but failed to become an Act before the General Election. Meanwhile, relations between the government and industry became much closer in various ways. The National Economic Development office had been set up by the Conservatives in 1962 with a charter to examine national economic performance. It was a tripartite organization of government, management and unions. This organization, which may be described as a well-meant substitute for economic planning, has never been disbanded.[19] While it is a useful forum it does not constitute a strain or provocation and functions smoothly without causing any serious reaction. Labor, upon taking office, concentrated on economic planning which culminated in a further reduction of the already vague distinction between industry in the private sector and industry in the public sector. More and more firms sought government assistance and soon found themselves, for all intents and purposes, under rigid government control.

The Conservative government, upon taking office in June 1970, planned to reduce industrial controls. The Industrial Reorganization Corporation was disbanded as was the Prices and Incomes Board. The Nationalized industries were to be scrutinized with a view to selling their fringe activities to the public sector.[20] Although committed to deregulation, the Heath government was quickly driven to reverse its proclaimed policy of cutting down the public sector and was compelled to extend it. The most dramatic case was the collapse of Rolls-Royce early in 1971. According to British economist C. D. Foster

"on February 17, 1971 Parliament
passed a short Act of one clause
which authorized Ministers to
spend an undefined sum in acquiring any part of the under-
taking and assets of Rolls-Royce
or any company which is a subsidiary part of it. This brief
and comprehensive Act is a most
dangerous precedent; no Labor
government has ever taken such
a momentous step." [21]

Of course, the government was faced with an
extremely difficult situation. The bankruptcy
of a company of the standing of Rolls-Royce
would have done irreparable harm to British prestige. The economy of Derby where Rolls-Royce
employed twenty-two thousand workers was imper-
illed; and this at a time of rising unemployment.
The take-over and the injection of public money
enabled a renegotiation of the Lockheed contract
for the RB.211 engine, which would otherwise
have collapsed. In these negotiations the government as financial backer played an important
role. [22]

It is unlikely that the government will
disengage itself from Rolls-Royce for some years
because of the company's need for long-term re-
financing and in-depth reorganization. As the
aerospace industry is so largely dependent on
government policy and finance, the final solution may be the merger of the Rolls-Royce aero-
engine section with some other firm in the industry. The car section which is far less important can no doubt be sold to a private industry. Under the Financial Assistance For Industry Act of 1972 the government again extended
its control over the public sector under provisions authorizing financial assistance to promote employment. The financing could be diverse
and even include the acquisition of a company or
of its shares. To operate this Act the government set up, under a Minister, an Industrial
Development Executive to work in conjunction
with the Department of Trade and Industry. It

is not surprising, therefore, that the Executive
has developed an outlook of his own and become
fairly independent as a disperser of government
assistance on a scale far beyond the scope of
the defunct Industrial Reorganization Corporation
of the sixties. It is clear that the threat of
high and rising unemployment has panicked the
Conservative government into causing this in-
credible about-face.

It looks likely, therefore, that during the
late seventies there will develop a much fuller
mixed economy in the United Kingdom than was
previously known. This is a revolution fraught
with great significance since government subsidies of enterprises have already adversely affected the economy. It is impossible to decide,
furthermore, if unemployment would have been
higher had the government not been so liberal
with financial help. What is quite definite,
however, is that the cost of maintaining employment in the nationalized industries by means of
this support has risen rapidly. Both workers
and management, knowing that eventually the
government will bail them out, make settlements
at too high a level. Inflation accelerates,
consequently, and costs increase far more than
is justified. This practice is spreading
widely over both the public and private sectors
to the degree that the boundary between the two
sectors has become indistinguishable.

As mentioned earlier the great victim of
post-war Socialism in Britain was the value of
the pound. Devaluation in 1949 was followed by
the stop-go crises of the fifties and early sixties and those in turn were followed by the delayed devaluation of 1967. The high level of
taxation and the prodigality with public funds
which marked both the Labor and the Conservative
administrations prompted a great increase in
the supply of money which in turn prompted rising prices and depreciation of the pound. The
latter was officially recognized in 1972 by the
official decision to float the pound, which
meant in effect a further devaluation of about
ten percent by early 1973.

TABLE 2

GREAT BRITAIN'S UNEMPLOYMENT RATES

1965 - 1975	1976 First Quarter
3.25%	6.30%
Of The Labor Force	Of The Labor Force

Source: FORTUNE Research, FORTUNE, August 1976, p. 131.

NOTE: It is apparent that GNP growth in Great Britain has been minimal. Consumer Prices, however, rose just in the first four months of 1976 a high twenty five percent. On the other hand, unit labor costs (in national currency) increased from 1970 to 1975 a whopping two hundred sixty four percent. Productivity, as reflected by the nation's output per manhour has now turned downwards. Furthermore, just in the first four months of 1976 the unemployment rate increased by ninety four percent. Milton Friedman said of Great Britain in 1978 that

> "It's going to continue to slide toward economic and financial collapse, in the sense that it will be more and more difficult for Britain to meet government expenditures without resorting to ever higher rates of inflation, without printing more money; it will be harder and harder for Britain to compete in the world at large. The standard of life of the ordinary Briton will go down. When this will end nobody knows, but one of these days that will result not only in a steady economic decline, but in a violent-- in a drastic political change. It will, almost inevitably, I believe, lead to complete loss of democracy and of freedom to the establishment of a collec-

TABLE 2 (Continued)

tivist totalitarian state. I
think if you want an example for
Britain that is highly relevant,
the experience of Chile with,
first, Allende and then the take-
over by a military junta is an
extremely pertinent experience.
That's the road Britain is going
down, and that is the ultimate
outcome. I don't know enough
about Britain to know who will
be the people who will take over;
whether it will be of the left,
the people who have Communist
leanings, Socialist leanings;
whether it will be some other
group. But that's the only outcome that is conceivable." 23

These developments were seriously aggravated by the workers in the nationalized industries (miners, railwaymen, electrical workers) who exploited their powerful position and forced the Government early in 1972 to capitulate to their excessive demands. As a result, the Government, driven desperate by the accelerating inflation, imposed a price and pay freeze in November 1972. This was followed by restrictions imposed on pay and on most prices until autumn 1973.[24]

By these measures the Conservative Government took control of industry and commerce on a scale never before reached in peacetime. But control is still most severe in the nationalized industries, which have become completely the creatures of government. Inflation has hit them with special severity, because their workers have secured increases in pay far beyond the capacities of the industries to bear and which therefore force them into deficits which are belatedly made good by government grants or subsidies. The value of the pound, consequently, continues to weaken from these post-war policies and there is a continuation of inflationary pressures. Drastic changes in priorities are required, not tinkering with symptoms which has been the practice to date. As recently reported in the Wall Street Journal the woes of the British economy are now well known and, it would appear, chronic. They include low productivity, recurrent balance of payments problems, a weak currency, high rates of inflation, inadequate growth of output, and disappointing living standards.[25] Since the early 1960's both British and foreign commentators have habitually blamed insufficient investment. Indeed, this diagnosis is practically standard in speeches of politicians and company chairmen, and in articles by economists and financial journalists.

A good case in point is the British Leyland financial failure. This company is Britain's last major homegrown auto manufacturer. Its deficiencies symbolize to the world the short-

comings of the country's industrial sector.
Leylands lavish spending performance, coupled
with a marked lack of management circumspection,
is added evidence of trouble governments get into when they try to rescue foundering private
enterprises. After the Company's financial collapse the National Enterprise Board, set up in
1975 by the Labor government as part of its industrial strategy, bought ninety five percent
of the corporation's shares. This action did
not, however, solve any fundamental problems.
Rather, it underlined the need for another
large infusion of investment capital by the
government to promote new development and advance new marketing strategies. Should British
Leyland go down again it is likely that the company would be either fully nationalized and per-
manently subsidized by the taxpayers or would be
placed into receivership thus intensifying unemployment and adversely affecting the British
balance of payments. Either recourse would be
calamitous.[26]

The belief that investment is good medicine
is by no means confined to Britain. Many Americans, including a fair number of conservative
businessmen, take it as axiomatic that the ultimate solution to economic problems is more investment. This belief is reflected in, for example, those recurrent demands in the United
States for increases in the investment tax
credit. But the merits of investment spending
as an instrument for increasing activity and
employment are unrelated to its productivity.
Keynes wrote explicitly that any net increase
in spending may serve the purpose of increasing
economic activity. This analysis was developed
by Keynes, however, with conditions of high
general unemployment in mind. He would surely
not have thought it applicable to the post-
war world. Even today, only six and one third
percent of the British labor force is unemployed. Yet references to inadequate investment as
a cause of the British disease[27] almost always
refer to investment in the Keynesian sense.
They refer, not to its quality or productivity,
but to its volume. At present the corrective

actions being undertaken to cure the British disease are under way. Under immense pressure from the United States and West Germany, the British labor government reluctantly agreed to adopt a package of spending cuts and tax hikes in exchange for a critically needed $3.9 billion loan from the International Monetary Fund. The agreement in principle was reached after a month of tense behind the scenes negotiations.[28]

Prime Minister James Callaghan in 1976 agreed to take the politically explosive step of carving $5.8 billion out of Britain's $18 billion deficit over the next two years, largely by slashing government outlays. The Cabinet considered draconian spending cuts, a moratorium on all government construction and the elimination of automatic cost of living increases from social security payments and civil service pensions. Defense expenditures were expected to be cut too, but not as sharply as social spending. Some British taxes would have to be raised. The levy which was most likely to be boosted was the value-added tax which is a super comprehensive sales tax.

Attempts to cut back on Britain's social services met raucous opposition from left-wing Laborites in Parliament. But the leftists did not gain enough support among opposing Liberals and Tories to have the spending cuts rejected. Britain did not have much choice. The pound had declined sharply through most of the year and foreign debts had fallen due. For example, about $1.6 billion had to be paid on an earlier loan from the Group of Ten (industrial nations). Britain's creditors, including Arab sheiks and international bankers, have grown increasingly skeptical about the country's ability to pay its way. Thus, after Whitehall applied for a loan in September 1976, the International Monetary Fund imposed stiff requirements as a condition for its investment.

The government's main concern was and still is low productivity, galloping inflation and gross overgrowth of the public sector. Inflation has dropped sharply due to North Sea oil revenues, some union wage restraint and a modest tax cut but the net effect on the British disease is hardly noticeable. British industry, in order to be more competitive, must shed still more workers than can be absorbed even in a healthy expanding industrial sector. Yet, once again an epidemic of strikes by rapacious unions is enfeebling Britain. This latest outbreak is posing the most serious threat yet to Prime Minister Margaret Thatcher's new Conservative government.[29]

Finally the Socialists today are bewildered, taking stock, and facing an uncertain future. For over half a century their movement was almost entirely devoted to the principle of controlled enterprise. Now that so much of their program has been realized in Great Britain's private and public sectors it has failed to live up to the promise of its doctrine. Britain's economy has faltered and it has had to look to the capitalistic sector for salvation. Yet capitalism in the United States also is beset by an inordinate amount of government regulation and its economy may one day suffer from the British malady. For a clear view of American enterprise we will investigate statutory controls exercised by the regulatory commissions and the private sector's counter actions to effect deregulation.

[1]Great Britain, Parliament, <u>Parliamentary Papers</u>, Cmnd. 6527, 1944, "White Paper on Employment Policy."

[2]R. Kelf-Cohen, <u>British Nationalisation 1945-1973</u>, (London: Macmillan St. Martin's Press, 1973), 15. For additional in depth study of events which influenced nationalization read G. D. H. Cole's <u>The Post-War Condition of Britain</u>, (New York: Praeger Publishers, 1957) and Adam B. Ulam's <u>Philosophical Foundations of English Socialism</u>, (Cambridge: Harvard University Press, 1951).

[3]J. M. Keynes, <u>The General Theory of Employment, Interest and Money</u>, (New York: Macmillan and Company, 1936), 379.

[4]<u>Ibid.</u>, 381.

[5]<u>Ibid.</u>, 382.

[6]R. Kelf-Cohen, <u>Twenty Years of Nationalisation</u>, (London: Macmillan St. Martin's Press, 1969), 285.

[7]H. T. N. Gaitskell, <u>Socialism and Nationalisation</u>, (London: Fabian Tract 300, 1956), 18-19.

[8]W. A. Robson, "Problems of Industrial Nationalisation," <u>Political Quarterly</u>, January 1969, 108.

[9]For intensive study of the Fabians read R.H.S. Crossman, editor, <u>New Fabian Essays</u>, (New York: Praeger Publishers, 1952) and Margaret Cole, editor, <u>The Webbs and their Work</u>, (New York: Frederick Muller, 1949).

[10]Great Britain, Parliament, <u>Parliamentary Papers</u>, The Coal Board's "Guillebaud Report," March 2, 1960.

[11]R. Kelf-Cohen, British Nationalisation 1945-1973, (London: Macmillan St. Martin's Press, 1973), 89.

[12]Robert Bacon and Walter Eltis, Britain's Economic Problem: Too Few Producers, (New York: St. Martin's Press, 1976), 101.

[13]Morley Safer and Milton Friedman, "Will There Always Be An England?" (New York: CBS News 60 Minutes Broadcast transcript, Volume IX, Number 10, November 28, 1976), A Scholarly overview may also be obtained by reading Leslie Hannah's The Rise of the Corporate Economy: The British Experience, (Baltimore: Johns Hopkins, 1976.

[14]R. Kelf-Cohen, British Nationalisation 1945-1973, (London: Macmillan St. Martin's Press, 1973), 254.

[15]Labour Party Policy Pamphlet No. 1, British Transport, n.d., "Industry and Society", 1957.

[16]Great Britain, Parliament, Parliamentary Papers, Cmnd. 4027, 1969, "Reply by Government on Ministerial Control of Nationalised Industries."

[17]Great Britain, Parliament, Parliamentary Papers, Cmnd. 3561, Prices and Income Board, "Proposals for Bus and Railway Fare Increases in London."

[18]Great Britain, Parliament, Parliamentary Papers, Cmnd. 3580, :Labour Government's Economic Record."

[19]Ibid., 21.

[20]R. Kelf-Cohen, British Nationalisation 1945-1973, (London: Macmillan St. Martin's Press, 1973), 259.

[21]C. D. Foster, Politics, Finance and the Role of Economics, (London: George Allen and Unwin, Ltd., 1972), 109.

[22]Ibid., 131.

[23]Morley Safer and Milton Friedman, "Will There Always Be An England?" (New York: CBS News 60 Minutes Broadcast Transcript, Volume IX, Number 10, November 28, 1976), 17. For an in-depth view of the complexities of the inflation phenomenon in Great Britain attention should be directed to John Flemming's Inflation, (New York: Oxford University Press, 1976).

[24]Robert Bacon and Walter Eltis, Britain's Economic Problem: Too Few Producers, (New York: St. Martin's Press, 1976), 98.

[25]Per Time magazine, p. 90, November 8, 1976, the pound in relation to the United States dollar, dropped in late October, 1976 to an all time low of 1.59 pounds versus 2.58 pounds in the summer of 1973.

[26]Robert Ball, "Saving Leyland Is A Job For Hercules," FORTUNE, July 3, 1978, 58-63.

[27]Morley Safer and Milton Friedman, "Will There Always Be An England?" (New York: CBS News 60 Minutes Broadcast Transcript, Volume IX, Number 10, November 28, 1976), 9.

[28]John Flemming, Inflation, (New York: Oxford University Press, 1976), 85.

[29]"Guidelines: The British Experience," Dun's Review, November 1978, 76-79. A critical account of British labor policies in this century, with a clear suggestion that the traditional prescriptions are no longer workable, is contained in David Howell's British Social Democracy, (New York: St. Martin's Press, 1976).

CHAPTER IV

UNITED STATES REGULATION OF ENTERPRISE:
A HISTORICAL OVERVIEW

In the twentieth century, the United States
government passed legislation setting up regulatory commissions authorizing the federal government to exercise controls over enterprise to an
unprecedented degree.[1] Ironically the government has had to regulate free enterprise in order to save it from abusive trade practices and
from concentrations of economic power which may
make the desired end of a free competitive system impossible. This action has affected economic growth adversely and beneficially. In all
instances, however, the overall result has, up
to the present, contributed positively to the
well-being of the nation and made capitalism an
appealing model for economic growth.

Regulatory agencies have the power to affect
both collective and individual endeavors, have
the power to prescribe generally what shall or
shall not be done in a given situation, to determine whether the law has been violated in a
particular case, to proceed against violators,
and even impose fines and render money judgments.
Agencies endowed with these powers are termed
regulatory because their activities impinge upon the rights of private individuals and regulate
the manner in which such rights may be exercised.
Their archetype is the Interstate Commerce Commission which was set up in 1887 to regulate
discriminatory rate fixing and destructive competition among railroads. In the ensuing years a
similar need for regulation presented itself in
other areas of the economy. The assertion of
government control in various fields led to the
setting up of agencies patterned after the first
regulatory commission. It was only natural that
machinery similar to that which had proved adequate in the regulation of railroads should be
used as the same basic problem arose in other
fields. The need for specialization to deal
with specialized problems of economic supervision
was met in the same way as it had been in 1887.

The almost inevitable nature of the post-Inter-
state Commerce Commission development was expressed by Elihu Root in 1916 when he wrote
that

>"there is one field of law develop-
>ment which has manifestly become
>inevitable. We are entering upon
>the creation of a body of adminis-
>trative law quite different in its
>machinery, its remedies, and its
>necessary safeguards from old me-
>thods of regulation by specific
>statutes enforced by the courts.
>As any community passes from
>simple to complex conditions the
>only way in which government can
>deal with the increased burdens
>thrown upon it is by the delega-
>tion of power to be exercised in
>detail by subordinate agents, sub-
>ject to the control of general di-
>rections prescribed by superior
>authority. The necessities of
>our situation have already led to
>an extensive employment of that
>method. The Interstate Commerce
>Commission, the state public ser-
>vice commissions, the Federal
>Trade Commission, the powers of
>the Federal Reserve Board, the
>health departments of the states,
>and many other supervisory offices
>and agencies are familiar illustra-
>tions."[2]

James Landis, a former dean of Harvard Law
School and noted scholar of administrative agencies, has written that, as particular industries
posited problems of abusive tactics with which
traditional legal devices had failed to cope,
this new method of control made its appearance.
He observed, also, that industries with sick-
nesses stemming from misdirection as to objec-
tive or from failure adequately to meet public
needs quickly came under the fostering guardianship of the state. The mode of the exercise of
that guardianship was the administrative pro-

cess.[3]

In 1973 the Federal Organization Manual
listed fifty-two independent administering agencies. The most important of these are the Civil
Aeronautics Board, the Federal Communications
Commission, the Federal Power Commission, the
Federal Trade Commission, the Interstate Commerce Commission, the National Labor Relations
Board, and the Securities and Exchange Commission. The decisions of these agencies, in their
respective areas of regulation, directly affect
the national economy and the quality, service
and prices paid by consumers in nearly every
category of commerce.[4] Their areas of regulation include transportation, carriers, utilities
and the investment business. They exercise
broad regulatory powers such as licensing and
rate fixing. In the area of unfair trade and
labor practices the applicable agency is given
discretionary authority to approve or prohibit
practices employed in business. This is the
primary power possessed by the Federal Trade
Commission and the National Labor Relations
Board. Similar authority is vested in the agencies which regulate given industries. These are
the Interstate Commerce Commission, the Civil
Aeronautics Board, the Federal Communications
Commission, the Federal Power Commission and the
Securities and Exchange Commission. Thus the
Interstate Commerce Commission must approve all
railroad consolidations, closures, and issuance
of stocks and bonds; it also has prohibitory
power over discriminatory and other improper
railroad practices. These powers, together with
that over rate fixing, tend to make the Commission a virtual superboard of directors of the
railroad industry. These are powers of immense
scope devised with little regard to constitutional theory. Since the "regulation of industry cannot be carried out effectively under a
rigid separation of powers, concentrated industrial power must be controlled by concentrated
governmental power."[5] The regulatory commissions, such as the Interstate Commerce Commission, have accordingly been made the repositories of all three types of governmental power:
legislative, administrative, and judicial. Ad-

ditionally, in many cases, regulatory authority has been conferred by the Congress upon the ordinary executive departments such as that of the Secretary of Agriculture who administers more than forty regulatory statutes. They concern stockyards and commodity exchanges.

From a legal point of view, there seems to be little difference in the two types of repositories of regulatory power. Those differences that do exist are in administration and in the relation of the independent regulatory commission to the principle of internal responsibility within the executive branch. These differences have militated against the use of the commission type of agency in all cases where regulatory power has been delegated. In fact the principle of ministerial responsibility in the British sense, i.e., executive accountability to the supreme legislature, is not a part of the American government system. The principle executive officers, on the other hand, are responsible to the President, the head of the executive branch. The President has absolute power of removal over the ordinary executive departments, and he can thus ensure that the policies administered by them are not in conflict with his views. The basic principle of ordinary governmental administration is that of the executive hierarchy, with the President at its head, possessing complete power of supervision and control. The position of the regulatory commission is very different. Independence is, indeed, an essential attribute to the Commerce Commission type agencies. These bodies are called the independent regulatory commissions because they are all located outside the three branches of government. They are not subject to the direct supervision or control of the President or of other officers in the executive branch.[6]

The independence of these commissions is partly the result of Congress' desire to keep all this power out of the hands of the executive branch, and partly a consequence of their exercise of powers which are judicial in nature.

All the commissions have power to decide disputed cases which greatly affect the rights and liberties of those who engage in the business controlled. This power is, doubtlessly, best exercised in an atmosphere of independence, rather than as part and parcel of the process of execution of the laws, exposed to all the pressures which play upon the political branches. The citizen has, therefore, some guarantee that his case will not be decided merely at the pleasure of the political executive.[7]

It should, at the same time, be recognized that the independence of the regulatory commissions tends to place difficulties in the way of executive coordination. If the policies pursued by the commissions conflict with those of the President, efficient government may be seriously impaired. It was their lack of accountability to the President which led an official report to describe the independent regulatory commissions as "in reality miniature independent governments set up to deal with the railroad problem, the banking problem, or the radio problem."[8] There are practical limitations in any legal principle which restricts the power of the President over officers appointed by him. Inherent in the highest office exists a power and prestige that few in Washington are able to withstand for, as a practical matter, the officials concerned owe their tenure to presidential pleasure. The members of the regulatory agencies can rarely, if ever, be withdrawn from the usual temptations of private interest, in the sense in which the judges can be. The President has, more often than not, been able to achieve his objectives in the regulatory commissions by means other than removal.

The regulatory agencies under discussion are all of the commission type. They are headed by a group of men, ranging in number from five to eleven, all having basically equal power. Their extensive policy-making functions may be seen from the breadth of the powers vested in them by enabling statutes which delegate authority in the broadest terms. Thus the In-

terstate Commerce Commission is empowered to
fix just and reasonable rates, the Federal
Trade Commission to eliminate unfair methods of
competition, the Securities and Exchange Commission to apply such concepts as maintenance
of a fair and orderly market and reasonable
rates of commission, and the National Labor Relations Board to prohibit unfair labor practices.

An outstanding example of a commission
vested with wide discretionary powers is the
Federal Communications Commission. In granting
a broadcast license or exercising any control
over broadcasting the Federal Communications
Commission need only to consider if public con-
venience, interest, or necessity will be served
thereby. In practice, the Congress has given
the commission what amounts to carte blanche.
Telling the Federal Communications Commission to
act in the public interest is the same as telling it to deal with the regulatory problem as
it chooses. It should be recognized, however,
that when the powers vested in an agency such as
the Federal Communications Commission give it
virtually uncontrolled life and death power over
the broadcasting industry, those engaged in
broadcasting simply cannot afford to risk having to live with a commission which is hostile
to them. The result has been constant efforts
on the part of the industry to influence the
commission, to ensure that it will favor their
interests.[9] Such attempts by the regulated to
control the regulators has presented problems
in all the commissions. At times these endeavors have been so successful that it has become a mere fiction to mask the reality of regulation for the benefit of the regulated. Recently Supreme Court Justice Warren Burger
noted that "the primary purpose of the regulatory commission was, of course, to protect the
consuming public."[10] The areas in which Congress has sought to regulate have had two essential characteristics. In the first place,
the businesses concerned displayed monopolistic
tendencies. This has been particularly true,
of course, in the public utility field where

monopoly is inherent in its nature. Even more important, perhaps, is the fact that the services provided by the regulated industries have been considered essential to the public.

These two factors have made regulatory intervention necessary. In its absence monopolistic tactics in the industry concerned lead to abusive practices before which the public is helpless. The resultant lack of effective competitive forces make it futile to depend on the normal working of the free market to protect the consumer. But as the service furnished is an essential one, the consumer has no alternative but to purchase it at the industry's terms. To redress the balance between industry and the consuming public, the state has stepped in through the medium of the regulatory agency.

The theory on which regulatory agencies should act was well expressed back in 1914 by Samuel O. Dunn, a leading Progressive of the period, when he stated that management of public utilities should be left in the hands of the owners or those they choose to represent them. He said, furthermore, that "the regulating commissions should be strong enough in personnel and statutory power to exercise corrective authority over the managements when the acts of the managements are unreasonable and unjust to the public."[11] This public interest application was intended when Congress created the regulatory system. By today's standards, however, the process is a failure and self-regulation has been substituted in its stead.

A number of astute observers of the regulatory process have called attention to what they have termed the life cycle of the regulatory agencies. According to them, each of the commissions has experienced roughly similar periods of growth, maturity and decline. The life cycle begins with the agency's birth, when the proponents of regulation have won their struggle for legislative recognition of their demands for reform. The reforming impetus carries over into the newly created commission,

and it is during the agency's youthful phase
that it is most vigorous in fighting for the
public interest. Young agencies are dominated
by the qualities of youth, energy, ambition,
and imagination. As time goes on, the commissions lose their youthful vigor, and administrative aggressiveness is replaced by apathy.
During the period of maturity those who are regulated give up their efforts to oppose regulation and instead direct their energies toward
taking over the regulatory body. In the agency,
youthful exuberance gives way to a desire to
avoid conflicts and to enjoy good relationships
with the regulated industry. It is during the
phase of its maturity that the regulatory commission tends more and more to equate the public interest with the interests of the regulated groups.[12]

   This tendency is carried to its logical
conclusion during the agency's period of old
age when, according to Arlene Hershman, noted
observer of regulatory agencies, "there de-
velops over the years a relationship between
the regulators and the regulated wherein they
have learned to live with each other and have,
in fact, grown intimately dependent on each
other."[13]

   Not all liberals have believed unquali-
fiedly in the modern type of regulatory statute.
"Of course," wrote the Supreme Court's Chief
Justice Holmes with characteristic candor to
his famous correspondent Sir Frederic Pollack
in 1910, "I enforce whatever constitutional
laws Congress or somebody else sees fit to
pass -- and do it in good faith to the best of
my ability -- but I don't disguise my belief
that the Sherman Act is a humbug based on economic ignorance and incompetence, and my dis-
belief that the Interstate Commerce Commission
is a fit body to be entrusted with rate-mak-
ing."[14] Many other observers have come to
share the great jurist's doubts concerning the
Interstate Commerce Commission. Perhaps its
most severe critic was Alfred E. Smith. "I
find little in recent history to justify the

continuance of the Interstate Commerce Commission as now organized," he declared in 1933. "What we need is a new transportation system, not endless hearings on a system that does not work."[15] Currently, a Ralph Nader-sponsored study of the Interstate Commerce Commission reflected the same thinking in its observation that "the ICC should be abolished in its present form. Because there has been much reliance on misguided ICC policies, change must come through planned stages. There is need for some of the function the ICC should be providing."[16]

More recently, the doubts about the effectiveness of regulation have extended to all of the federal regulatory commissions. Despite this, the regulatory agency has come into its own as a primary government institution and the Interstate Commerce Commission has become the model of agency organization and administration.

The regulatory agency was the governmental instrument of the New Deal. Through it, Washington hoped to work a progressive modification of the economy and the society, comparable, at the very least, to the great English Reform Movement of the last century. Many even saw in the regulatory process the ultimate replacement of private industry, which would take over the role of economic leadership in the public interest. This was, according to Louis Jaffe, noted judicial scholar, the ultimate view that enthralled the extreme New Dealer; this was the specter that terrified the world of private industry.

After noting the rise of the regulatory process, Justice Felix Frankfurter stated that, "Concerning its efficacy, however, pessimism has supplanted the earlier feeling of hope." What is clear is that the rise of the regulatory agency has meant a drastic shift in the legal center of gravity, so far as lawmaking is concerned. The legislature has continued to enact an increasing number of laws, and the courts to apply them, in an ever mounting number of decisions. Legislative and judicial lawmaking have come to be dwarfed by the administrative law-making function. In fact, Howard J. Morgens, chairman of the Proctor & Gamble board of directors' executive committee, has written that the picture during this century has been one of the increasing ineffectiveness in the administration of regulatory laws. He said that "though the regulatory manner has been ordinary, that has scarcely affected the concentration of regulatory power that has characterized this era."[17] One of the notable features of contemporary law has been the continuing growth of administrative authority. This is all the more striking because the present period has seen a climax in the disillusionment with the regulatory agency that had begun even before mid-century.

To speak of public institutions as endowed with life is not mere metaphor. The government body, like the animal, has its periods of vigor and decline. The vital spark appears to have gone out of the regulatory agencies. Even undue partisan-motivated influence and corruption have begun to appear. Yet, not only is there no effective movement to reduce administrative power; if anything, the trend is still all the other way. Currently the administering of massive government control is being inflicted on the oil industry prime source of the nation's energy. Oil, therefore, is no longer merely fuel. It has become the rationale for establishing a whole new federal regulatory bureaucracy. Additionally and, more importantly, it is now used as a weapon of national and international policy and is, thus, playing a decisive role in the global marketplace. In this role oil is now the subject of endless debates, countless publications and studies, and world political-economic reorganization to cope with the related energy crisis. All of this represents constant and concentrated interference in the operation of the free enterprise system and appears to discourage continued private investment in the economy.

Now, after more than forty years of increasing government interference into business activities, the American economy has become a mixed economy in which government dominates but business is still impelled toward efficiency by the pursuit of profit. Regulations are a growing and permanent reality. If the government continues to expand its reach into business, the system might not survive. This worry is prevalent among American business executives who consider regulatory agencies as a new fourth branch of government with power out of all relationship to their charter. Some agencies are highly effective. Many others, however, are living, breathing anachronisms which, through congressional protection, have avoided extinction. Apart from sheer waste federal regulation has contributed to higher and higher inflation in many ways. Some agencies almost automatically grant requests for rate increases by the regulated industries. These increases are synonymous with rising prices. Added to this is the high cost factor of the incredibly voluminous paperwork imposed on the regulated by the regulators.

One of the most costly components of regulation involves the waiting time for the issuance of a rule. Although affected parties are usually interested in a particular outcome their main concern is obtaining a timely decision. Any decision even if wrong and/or for altogether wrong reasons! Time is needed to plan and, therefore, uncertainty is an expensive commodity.[18]

Nevertheless, it must be recognized that some government intervention is necessary in order to prevent abusive and unscrupulous business practices. In addition, there must be periodic updates and reviews to assure that such regulation adapts to changing conditions. Upon examination it may be advisable to eliminate certain agencies, to adopt administrative and organizational changes in others, and to step up antitrust enforcement in some areas. Such conclusions would meet strong opposition, of course, from affected interest groups including certain members and committees of Congress. Indeed, Congress itself has been woefully deficient in pursuing reform. For this reason, a

disciplined approach as well as a comprehensive
one becomes necessary. All special arrangements
must be reconsidered. It is essential that all
the cards be face up. Sweetheart relationships
must be reassessed because it should be clearly
understood that the unexamined agency is simply
not worth keeping. Not even at the expense of
losing some benefits or being encumbered with
uncomfortable restrictions. If the task is approached with perseverance and integrity there
will no doubt be substantial benefits for the
economy and for society as a whole!

We have determined that the prerequisites
for a free enterprise system are now well-de-
fined. They include: (a) private property, (b)
free access to all money and capital sources,
(c) free exchange of goods and services to meet
the demands of the marketplace, and (d) free development of managerial activities, intensified
by competition within the framework of existing
regulatory laws. There then should be no need
for the further extension of regulatory power
over the oil industry especially when it appears
that such encroachment might well reduce the industry's motivation for economic growth.

FOOTNOTES

[1]Robert E. Cushman, The Independent Regulating Commissions, (New York: Oxford University Press, 1941, reprinted by Octagon Books, 1972).

[2]U. S. Congress, Senate, Interstate Commerce Act, S. Doc. 1093, 49th Cong., 2d Sess., February 4, 1887.

[3]American Bar Association Reports, 41/368. To review procedures of regulatory law in greater detail read "The Reformation of American Administrative Law" by Richard Stewart, in the Harvard Law Review, June 1975.

[4]James Landis, The Administrative Process, (Cambridge, Massachusetts: Harvard University Press, 1938), 14.

[5]Sen. Charles H. Percy, "A Prescription for Curing Our Regulatory Ills," Nation's Business, December 1976, 25.

[6]Morris P. Florina, Congress--Keystone of the Washington Establishment (New Haven: Yale University Press, 1977), 51.

[7]Bernard Schwartz, ed., The Economic Regulation of Business and Industry, A Legislative History of the U. S. Regulatory Agencies, vol. 1, (New York: Chelsea House Publishers, 1973), 7.

[8]Report of the President's Committee on Administrative Management, No. 39, 1937.

[9]Arlene Hershman, "Regulating The Regulators," Dun's Review, January 1977, 34.

[10]"Office of Communication v. Federal Communications Commission", 359 F. 2d 994, 1003-04, D. C. Cir., 1966. See also "What the Supreme Court Is Really Telling Business" by Walter Guzzard, Jr., in FORTUNE, January 1977.

[11]John Kenneth Galbraith, Economics and the Public Purpose, (Boston: Houghton Mifflin Company, 1973), 219.

[12]To review the much criticized behavioral aspects of the regulatory agencies in the light of the need for reform read Regulatory Reform Highlights, a study edited by W. S. Moore and published by (Washington, D. C.: American Enterprise Institute for Public Policy Research, 1976). Also see Regulatory Reform: A survey of Proposals in the 94th Congress, a Round Table Discussion, moderated by Eileen Shanahan and published by (Washington, D. C.: American Enterprise Institute for Public Policy Research, 1976).

[13]Arlene Hershman, "Regulating the Regulators," Dun's Review, January 1977, 35.

[14]Marver H. Bernstein, Regulating Business by Independent Commission, (Princeton: Princeton University Press, 1966), 89.

[15]Robert D. Fellmeth, The Interstate Commerce Omission, (New York: Grossman Publishers, 1970), 324.

[16]Ibid., 295.

[17]Howard J. Morgens, "A Third Century Look at the Balance Between Government and Business," Nation's Business, October 1976, 29.

[18]Marver H. Bernstein, Regulating Business By Independent Commission,(Princeton: Princeton University Press, 1966), 104.

CHAPTER V

THE OILFLATION, STAGFLATION EQUATION

An assessment of the energy situation in the United States, which gave birth to a whole new body of regulatory actions, is directly identified to the oil industry. In October, 1973, Arab states placed an embargo on oil shipments to the United States. All at once the nation had to go on daylight savings time, throttle back on the highways, and turn down thermostats. Millions of Americans found themselves lining up, sometimes for hours, at filling station pumps. Up to that moment they considered the Middle East as strictly a British problem. Now suddenly the impact of events had an adverse effect on their personal well-being. Oilflation (inflation triggered by steadily rising oil prices) had begun.

Oil got the United States deeply involved in the Middle East and caused widespread concern about the sudden emergence of an energy problem. This crisis appears to have been the result, primarily, of various policies of federal, state, and local governments. For years policymakers have been sacrificing the country's long-run interest to secure various short-run objectives, such as unrealistically low prices, wasteful patterns of consumption, and the too rapid application of environmental controls and restrictions.[1] This is especially true of policies toward fossil fuels. For example, primarily because of regulation of wellhead prices, exploration, development, and production of natural gas has fallen. As a result, customers who would normally consume natural gas were forced to switch to the nearest substitute fuel, which was usually oil.[2]

Yet, at a time when America had to intensify its efforts to find more oil to meet increased consumption it, instead, lowered the depletion allowance, withdrew leases for environmental reasons, delayed leasing of the outer continental shelf, blocked construction of the Alaskan pipeline, and, what is particularly relevant, im-

posed stringent price controls on the industry.
As a result, domestic production of oil failed
to keep pace with the extraordinary demands
placed upon it and Americans became increasingly
dependent on imported oil and particularly, oil
from the Middle East. This dependence posed major foreign policy and economic problems for the
United States and discouraged the building of
refineries primarily because of an uncertain supply of crude oil. This too forced reliance on
imported refined products as well as imported
crude oil and made the nation doubly vulnerable.
As a consequence of this dependence in fact, several countries actually curtailed exports to the
United States after Middle East fighting began,
but prior to the Arab boycott, in order to protect their own supplies and to minimize domestic
price increases.

The Arab oil embargo was lifted but the
energy problem is far from over and the United
States must correct the basic policies that have
made it susceptible to foreign supply disruptions.[3] The referenced policies are quite ir-
rational and include controls over the prices of
crude oil and refined products. These were followed by a succession of additional controls over
home heating oil and other distillates such as
gasoline, diesel oil, kerosene and kero/naphtha-
based jet fuel. In late 1972 the United States
began to experience shortages of No. 2 fuel oil.
One reason for this was an unusually cold and wet
fall, which resulted in extraordinary demand for
distillates for heating and crop drying. Another
reason was that the price of No. 2 oil and gasoline had remained virtually constant at mid-1971
levels throughout 1972.[4] As a direct result of
the freeze refiners requesting separate price increases for these products were almost invariably
turned down. In fact, several oil companies were
told that a price increase for a product would
require public hearings and lead to protracted
delays. The industry, therefore, took the course
of least resistance; it increased the price of
imported oil which was not subject to domestic
price control.

Adding to the problem was the use of diesel oil by No. 2 fuel oil consumers since this oil is chemically identical and was in good supply, while No. 2 fuel oil was short. These fuel oil consumers, mainly electric utilities, were paying diesel oil's related highway taxes for the privilege of its use and passing these taxes on to customers in the form of higher electricity rates. This experience was to have an imprint on future price controls. Subsequently the special treatment of visible products would continue, however, diesel oil would be treated identically with No. 2 fuel oil.

From January 11 to June 13, 1973 certain profit margin standards were developed for industry and labor, with the government monitoring compliance. Consequently, relief from profit margin limitations was given to firms that restricted price increases to less than one and a half percent per year. Immediately there followed a sharp jump in prices, particularly in home heating oil. This was, in part, a response to the early rigidities of regulations. It was also a result of market conditions, and the developing shortage of oil on a world-wide scale. As a result there was heavy criticism by Congress, the press, and various segments of the public of the government's handling of the controls program. There was also criticism of the industry which was already being blamed for shortages of home heating oil. Responding to these criticisms, the Cost of Living Council held hearings into the oil price increases and ruled that the twenty-three largest oil companies were to restrict their price increases. It also prohibited these companies from increasing product prices if their profits were over the base margin levels.[5] Because virtually all of these companies had foreign operations which were earning significantly higher profits, most of the twenty-three companies were already exceeding their base profit margins. The majors were, therefore, effectively prohibited from passing higher foreign crude oil or refined products costs on to their customers.

During the spring of 1973 the world supply of crude oil and refined products began to be tight. Consequently prices of foreign oil started to rise above the United States levels. Import prices also increased because of devaluation of the dollar. Because price control rulings were imposed at a time when world prices were rising rapidly, they became a potential deterrent to imports.[6] Perhaps the best example of distortion created by the controls is the experience with propane which is a close substitute for natural gas. Most propane is supplied by major oil companies who purchase it from small producers to supplement the propane manufactured in their refineries and produced in their natural gas processing plants. To avoid the price squeeze some of the major oil companies' propane supplies were diverted by the producers to brokers, utilities, manufacturing firms and other companies not subject to this price control. In 1973 the supply of natural gas was falling rapidly in response to the Federal Power Commission's restrictive price controls. Unduly low prices for natural gas, thus increased the demand for propane and effectively reduced its supply by discouraging production of propane associated with the production of natural gas. Most customers were willing and able to pay extremely high prices for propane. Utilities are, under existing regulations, generally permitted to roll these prices into their rate base. Also, industrial firms whose fuel costs are only a small proportion of their total costs can afford to pay very high prices for propane as an alternative to shutting down plants because of curtailments of natural gas. Given the developing shortage of natural gas, the price of propane would have risen irrespective of controls. Under the rulings, however, traditional customers were effectively denied the right to pay that price in order to purchase propane through their historical distributors, the major oil companies. As a result, these traditional customers, mostly farmers and low-income families dependent on propane for heating, experienced serious shortages.[7]

The Cost of Living Council's reaction to these shortages was a reversal of its policy toward propane and authorization to the major oil companies to increase prices to include a disproportionate share of their cost increase. As a consequence, propane prices soared far beyond levels necessary to assure adequate supplies, production increased, demand fell, and by the spring of 1974 propane was in surplus. Controls also hastened the destruction of the quota system for importing crude oil. Under the old mandatory oil import program, refiners were authorized specified levels of imports of crude oil. The amount of imports was determined by a sliding scale giving small refiners disproportionately high import quotas. As long as the world price of crude oil was below the domestic price the small refiner could swap with a major oil company his right to import crude oil for the domestic crude oil he needed to run his refinery. In 1973, however, world prices were rising while domestic prices were effectively frozen. Consequently, the value of import quotas fell sharply.

Adding to the difficulties of the independent, major oil companies had little incentive to import and exchange crude oil. Instead they sold it abroad in order to maximize their profits.[8] This led to two basic changes in the way crude oil was marketed in the United States. The first change was that many small refiners, denied the domestically produced crude oil they needed, successfully lobbied for an allocation program under which they would obtain their fair share of this product. The second change was that the price of domestic crude oil began to rise, a development that would eventually help to revive what had been a declining and moribund drilling industry.

The controls permitted the continuance of the incentive for major oil companies to transfer refined products from wholesale to retail markets, in this way circumventing price ceilings. At the same time, shortages of refined products brought about by a failure to build sufficient new refinery capacity in recent years also helped to dry up bulk sales of gasoline to municipalities and other traditional wholesale purchasers and to deepen the difficulties of various groups of independent marketers, particularly independent gasoline stations and fuel oil distributors purchasing on the spot market. Together, these developments generated what were to prove irresistible demands for allocation of oil by the government.[9]

Let us recognize that the major reason for this problem was failure by the industry to build new refineries or to expand existing refineries since the mid-1960's. This was due in part to excess refinery capacity and partly to various policies of federal, state, and local governments which discouraged new refinery construction. Because by 1973 United States refining capacity was limited, there was little excess production for sale at distressed prices. However, the price controls did, as it were, turn the knife in the back of the independent spot-market and wholesale purchaser. One way the majors increased profits without increasing prices was to switch gasoline and distillate from spot market to regular customers and from bulk to retail purchasers.

Also, the controls required the major oil companies to sell distillate and gasoline at prices which were low relative to other products, thus forcing them to undersell even those independent marketers who, by more efficient marketing techniques, should have continued to enjoy a competitive advantage in the absence of a spot market for oil.[10] Most independent marketers could continue to operate, but only by purchasing and selling their gasoline at higher prices relative to the major oil companies. In other words, independents began to lose what had been their stock in trade, their ability to sell at cut-rate prices. Eventually some of them were selling the highest-priced gasoline in the marketplace, while the heavily controlled outlets of the major oil companies cut their prices. Price controls, therefore, had far-reaching consequences to the competitive position of the independent marketers. Most of them continued to survive during the periods of shortages in spite of selling at relatively high prices. They did so, however, only by incurring long-term damage to their reputations. This is why, for example, a group of independent gasoline marketers from Georgia who petitioned the government for help in mid-1973 had as their principal request deregulation of the retail prices of major oil company outlets. The independents were concerned, correctly, that they would lose their reputation with the public as the price cutters of the industry and that this, in turn, would undermine their long-term position in the marketplace.[11]

New rules and another oil price freeze were effected in mid-1973. Physical commingling of imported and domestic products in storage or pipelines was still prevented even though separation was considered necessary to the effective monitoring of program compliance. These rules posed a dilemma for oil companies that operated in both foreign and domestic markets. If they were to sell higher priced imported products at the purchase price and lower priced domestic oil at the freeze price, which customers would be penalized and which would be favored? The Cost of Living Council's regulations in effect forced these companies to violate the Robinson-Patman Act, which requires non-discriminatory pricing among customers for the same class of product sold in the same marketplace. It also added to the then widespread criticism of the majors by these customers who, correctly or not, perceived that they were being discriminated against. On August 13, 1973 the Federal Energy Office was created, the Cost of Living Council was abolished and regulations were improved. One of the most significant improvements was the promulgation of a provision allowing imported oil to be commingled with domestic oil and sold at a weighted average price. Initially the new regulations were directed at the major oil companies, the producers and the marketers. The basic means of control was the ceiling price. It was thought that ceiling prices at the retail level would exert backward pressures on wholesale prices charged at the refinery level. Similarly, it was thought that a ceiling on prices received by refiners would exert backward pressures on prices paid to producers. The opposite happened; prices increased at the wholesale level forced retailers into a profit squeeze.[12]

In an effort to encourage new production a price system was established for crude oil whereby imports could be priced at cost and new domestic crude oil was freed from controls in order to seek the import price level. New crude oil was defined as production above the level of that achieved during 1972. The new pricing system was designed to increase domestic crude oil production by raising the crude price at the margin while allowing the lower average price to determine refined product prices. The results of this scheme were spectacular. The old crude oil ceiling price had become five dollars and twenty-five cents; the price of new oil was over ten dollars, a level more than enough to provide adequate incentive for new production. Drilling activity became intense and by March 1974 had risen by forty percent above its level one year earlier. As a result of the new price regulations nearly forty percent of all domestic oil in the United States had been deregulated.

Although the crude oil program encouraged new exploration and development, it also resulted in significant price differentials between the products of competing refiners. This, in turn, contributed to the difficulties of those refiners and marketers who, by happenstance, sold refined products manufactured from higher priced crude oil. The sharp rise in crude oil prices therefore, led to strong criticism and concentrated effort, by certain members of Congress and some segments of the public, to have laws enacted for their immediate rollback. At the same time, producer interests strongly opposed any administration ceiling or rollback of deregulated crude oil prices.[13] What was, thus, to have been a flexible ceiling price on old oil became, instead, an inflexible freeze price. This, then, resulted in very substantial pressures, particularly by refiners who historically relied

68

heavily on imported crude for price allocation,
for an extension of the existing allocation program to assure equitable sharing of priced crude
oil throughout the industry. Interests that had
previously fought to obtain special privileges
from the government to import low-priced oil from
the Middle East, Venezuela, and Canada were now
trying to obtain domestic oil at five dollars
and twenty-five cents under federal allocation
program.[14]

The pricing system invited manipulation.
For example, the fact that both old oil and new
oil could not be distinguished one from the other
upon emergence from a pipeline made it impossible
to police the system. This gave rise to unfoun-
ded reports of a refiner making an agreement with
a producer to purchase one barrel of new oil for
ten thousand dollars provided all of the producer's old oil was also included in the transaction. The ten thousand dollar price for a barrel
of oil was probably exaggerated. There were instances, however, of fifteen dollar and eighteen
dollar prices; prices above free market levels.
This resulted in consideration by the new Federal
Energy Administration(formerly the Federal Energy
Office) in May 1974 of ways to redefine price re-
ulations so that deregulated crude oil could sell
only at a fair market price designated by them.[15]

Some of the pricing system manipulations
generated real costs to society. For example,
there were reports of adjoining leaseholds agree-
ing to shut down some wells and of other unnecessary wells being drilled, thus increasing the
production of new oil on paper if not in fact.
There were also marginally legal ways of converting old oil to new oil merely by shuffling paper and redefining leaseholds. This latter method had the advantage of minimizing unnecessary
real costs of freeing a producer from price controls. The price of new oil is now far above
that necessary to encourage investment in drilling activity. As a result, the drilling industry has been faced with a number of bottlenecks,
including shortages of tubular steel, drilling
equipment and skilled personnel. Naturally, one

cannot expect an industry that was essentially moribund for over a decade to respond immediately to the price incentives it is now receiving.[16]

The government has also established a separate pricing system for refined products. Companies that market refined products, or products refined from imported crude oil, are finding that they are not competitive compared to companies that are fortunate enough to market products refined from domestically produced old crude oil. This competitive disadvantage of certain companies will become more acute as crude supplies increase.[17]

Despite the fact that it is stimulating new production, the existing price system is creating serious problems for the industry and the country. It is undermining the competitiveness of particular segments of the oil industry and increasing demands for the breakup of the major oil companies. It is forcing the major oil companies to behave like monopolists, undercutting the prices of some of their smaller, independent competitors. In the long run, there had to be a single price for the same product in the same marketplace. Price of both crude oil and refined products had to increase to levels that reflect import prices. Until this was done pricing problems would continue, pressures for price allocation would mount, and lobbying in Washington would remain the primary means of conducting business in the oil industry.[18]

While the producers' response to price regulations was accommodation, the marketers were openly hostile. This meant trouble for the Federal Energy Administration. Distributors and marketers are politically the most powerful segment of the industry. Once again drafters of regulations thought that by imposing ceilings on retail prices control could also be exerted on wholesale prices charged by refiners and large distributors. Regulations contained other provisions that were also particularly offensive to the independent retailers. As a result one thousand heating oil distributors and two thousand

gasoline dealers marched on Washington in pro-
test.[19] Substantial pressures were brought to
bear on the administration and Congress, with the
result that the price regulations affecting the
retail outlets were changed four times within the
space of a month, each change progressively more
favorable to the retail segment of the industry.
Congress then passed legislation which banned regulations discriminating against independent purchasers within the same class of trade. Regulations were next used to require that other products carry more than their fair share of raw
material costs. This created inequities which
caused propane prices to increase between two
hundred and four hundred percent. Since propane
was in exceedingly short supply the result was
extreme hardship for segments of the population
which used large amounts of propane.[20] These
included low-income families, particularly in
the South and Southwest and in relatively isolated areas. They also included farmers, who use
propane not only for heating but also for drying
crops. There were two major consequences of the
exorbitant propane price increases. One was a
sharp drop in demand and increase in production,
with the result that supply shortages were completely reversed. The propane price increases
also resulted in pressure for a price rollback.
Consequently, propane is now being treated as a
special product upon which only a limited amount
of raw material cost increases can be passed
through in the form of price increases. This
has raised special products from seventy five to
eighty percent of the refinery yield. The re-
maining other products, such as asphalt, jet
fuel, petrochemical feedstocks, and lubricating
oils must now bear an even greater share of raw
material cost increases.

Nevertheless, the ingenuity of the industry
prevails. Those whose day to day lives are devoted to the oil business continue to find ways
of modifying or adjusting to the policies of the
government. In order to comply with the price
control system, each major oil company and many
independents employ as many individuals as the
government does in attempting to administer the

program. There is a fundamental military principle that applies to current federal practice.
When the enemy is more knowledgeable, fighting
on its own soil, better motivated, better equip-
ped and more numerous the only alternative is
retreat.

In reviewing the great number of problems
created by price controls on oil and how these
problems have affected various aspects of the oil
business and the economy we have neglected the
most serious problem that controls have created;
the discouragement of investment in new productive capacity and industry in exploration and
development. The major reason the industry has
failed to build new refineries in recent years
has been uncertainty. This uncertainty has been
caused by, among other things, frequent changes
in government policies, including environmental
standards and regulations, tax laws, and restrictions on oil imports as well as changes in price
policies. It is recognized, of course, that
some uncertainty is a natural part of business
operations. Profits are, after all, a return to
the businessman who is willing to take risks.
The uncertainties created by price controls and
other government policies have, however, been
unnatural. These uncertainties have delayed
new investment in the United States and, because of this increased dependence upon high
cost, unstable foreign sources of oil.[21]

A summary of the consequences of price controls on the industry reveals that, despite the
intentions of the government, price controls
forced some major oil companies to undersell
their independent competitors. In addition production, distribution and consumption patterns
became distorted and costs to consumers increased steadily. The controls also increased
costs incurred by customers, encouraged unpro-
ductive and illegal activities by certain segments of the industry and discouraged imports
and high cost United States production.[22] They
disrupted the propane industry, reduced the use-
fulness of the Consumer Price Index as a measure
of inflation, encouraged the use of political

influence to maximize profits and, to some
extent, discouraged new investment in the industry. It appears, then, that the only useful
purpose of controls was to create the illusion
that the American government was doing something
to protect consumers from inflation. Meanwhile,
stagflation (inflation in a stagnant economy)
was born. This unfamiliar phenomenon would require new remedies.

In Europe and Japan governments were more
rational in their approach to oil price rises.
Since these countries are entirely dependent on
imports they simply paid the higher prices without following the foolish American policy of
holding down the price for old oil by direct
controls administered by a monstrous, wasteful,
inefficient and self-perpetuating bureaucracy
which, by its actions, played into the hands of
the Organization of Petroleum Exporting Countries (OPEC).[23] Nevertheless, here too, and
throughout the industrialized world, inflation
has become a pervasive and pernicious economic
fact of life. It is no respecter of ideologies
or political economic systems and has become an
international problem imported and exported
through the various channels of global trade and
finance. Since 1973 the world has been trying
to cope with this calamitous condition which was
sparked by the sudden oil price explosion. It
is a state of affairs which will not soon go
away. Its almost alarming results are the sustained depreciation of the United States dollar
against some major European currencies and the
Japanese yen during 1977 and the early part of
1978 and the ushering in of a new element of
instability in the already unstable international monetary system. One of the most critical
outcomes of dollar devaluation has been a new
and unwelcome pressure on the real price of
crude oil which is steadily shrinking despite
increased market prices. One wonders how long
OPEC will tolerate continued declines in the exchange value of their substantial oil export
earnings and the erosion of their dollar-denomi-
nated assets. Its officials continue to raise

TABLE 3

THE INFLATIONARY EXPLOSION OF INTERNATIONAL LIQUIDITY
(in billions of U.S. dollars)

	End 1969	End 1972	Mid-1978
Foreign Dollar Claims	78	146	373
On U.S. Government and Banks	49	85	221
On Foreign Branches of U.S. Banks	29	61	152
International Monetary Reserves	79	159	330
Foreign Exchange	34	104	256
1. Dollars & Eurodollars	20	81	
2. Other Currencies	7	15	
3. Other	7	8	
Other: World Monetary Gold, SDR Allocations and IMF Loans and Investments	46	55	75
Commercial Banks Foreign Liabilities in:	121	217	700
Dollars and Eurodollars	94	157	
Other Currencies	27	60	

SOURCES: These estimates are derived from tables published by the International Monetary Fund in its Annual Reports, by the Federal Reserve Bulletin, and by the Bank for International Settlements in its Annual Reports and quarterly releases on Eurocurrency and other international banking developments. They are not fully comparable due to the different definitions of foreign liabilities in U.S. and European reporting.

74

the market price of oil yet the outcome for OPEC
as a whole depends on the duration of the dollar
downswing, the currencies against which the depreciation is measured, the weight of such currencies in a basket and other trade-related factors. Thus, in terms of the value of Special
Drawing Rights, in which the dollar has a thirty-
three percent weight, the depreciation of United
States currency was about seven percent in 1977
and the early part of 1978. When counterbalanced
to the average change in dollar value in terms of
OPEC's imports the average decline during the
same period was nearly eighteen percent. The implications of these statistics are not of vital
concern to OPEC members, but are of serious por-
tent to the viability and efficiency of the international monetary system. The weakening
dollar, though it has a slow beneficial effect
on America's balance of payments, aggravates
inflation, encourages the flight of capital from
the United States and discourages private domestic investments. Above all the failing dollar
upsets the entire fragile fabric of the international monetary system.[24]

It appears that, since inflation begins with
monetary expansion, monetary contractions should
stop it in its tracks. "There is no technical
problem about how to end inflation," Nobel economist Milton Friedman has pointed out. "The real
obstacles are political." Immediate corrective
measures currently taken in the United States
include the imposition of inflation guidelines
on industrial labor contracts, deregulation of
airlines, trucking and railroads and intensive
efforts to develop additional alternative energy
supplies such as nuclear, geo-thermal, solar and
synthetic sources. In the long run, however, the
only real hope for dollar stability and OPEC cooperation is United States continued pursuit of
free trade and exchange policies and determined
market intervention to smooth out disorderly currency rates thus permitting other major currencies to serve as reserves along with the dollar.
Beyond these measures is a certain requirement
for enhanced coordination of policies among the
major industrial countries to ensure orderly non-

TABLE 4

THE U.S. BALANCE OF PAYMENTS
(in billions of U.S. dollars)

	1970	1975	1976	1977	Yearly Rate Sept-Dec. 1977	Jan-March 1978
Current Account	2	18	4	-15	-28	-27
Net Capital Outflows	5	14	12	18	11	13
Official Reserves and Bank Assets	-3	4	-8	-33	-39	-41
U.S. Assets	-2	14	24	12	35	24
1. Bank Loans	1	14	21	11	35	25
2. Official Reserves	-3	1	3	-	-	-1
U.S. Liabilities (-) to	-2	-10	-32	-44	-74	-65
1. Private Holders	6	-3	-14	-7	-11	-2
2. Official Holders:	-8	-7	-18	-37	-62	-63
OPEC	...	-7	-10	-7	-4	-7
Other	...	-	-8	-30	-58	-55
Dollar Depreciation (-) since May 1970, vis-a-vis ten major currencies (Percent).	-1	-15	-13	-19	-19	-22

SOURCE: Survey of Current Business, U. S. Department of Commerce, Washington, D. C.

NOTE: Minus signs indicate a decline of assets or an increase of liabilities. Capital outflows exclude official and bank assets liabilities. They reflect the recycling use of the dollar as an international parallel currency.

TABLE 5

HIGHLIGHTS OF EXTENT OF INFLATION
IN
SELECTED INDUSTRIAL COUNTRIES

| YEAR | INFLATION RECORD 1968-1977 (% CHANGE CONSUMER PRICE INDEX) | | | |
	UNITED STATES	GREAT BRITAIN	JAPAN	ALL INDUSTRIAL COUNTRIES
1978*	7.0	11.5	8.0	7.5
1977	6.5	15.0	7.4	7.0
1976	5.8	16.5	9.3	7.0
1975	9.1	24.2	11.8	N/A
1974	11.0	16.0	24.5	N/A
1973	6.2	9.2	11.7	N/A
1972	3.3	7.1	4.8	N/A
1971	4.3	9.5	6.3	N/A
1970	5.9	6.4	7.3	N/A
1969	5.4	5.5	5.6	5.0
1968	4.2	4.7	5.6	4.0

*Economic Forecasts
Sources: OECD Economic Outlook, No. 22, December 1977 and the Economist Intelligence Unit, Ltd., Quarterly Economic Reviews, IV Quarter 1977.

N/A: Not Available

inflationary growth under free market conditions. Also, equally essential, is an accommodative arrangement between OPEC and major oil consumers in relation to oil revenues and protection of purchasing power of the dollar.[25]

The pursuit of common objectives such as these necessitates sacrifices of sovereignty by government through the coordination of domestic money and tax policies. The people on the other hand, must recognize that continued deficit spending, upward pressures on wages without accompanying productivity increases and downward inflexibility of wages and prices during periods of excess labor and productive capacity combine to intensify inflation. Continued growth accompanied by higher living standards have proven themselves to be the rewards of a free competitive system. Nowhere is this better exemplified than in Japan which, since World War II, has emerged as a major industrial nation. We could perhaps benefit from a study of the Japanese industrial miracle.

FOOTNOTES

[1]Carl Solberg, "The Tyranny of Oil," American Heritage, Volume XXVIII, No. 1, December 1976. For a clear picture of OPEC's origins, actions and prospects, including the wresting of control of Mideast oil from the multinational corporations, read OPEC: Success and Profits, by Dankwart A. Rustow and John F. Mugno, (New York: New York University, 1976).

[2]Another substitute is electricity. However, most of the incremental output, particularly on the East Coast, is generated by burning oil. To obtain full coverage of environmentalists' views of energy problems read Energy and Human Welfare, three volumes edited by Barry Commoner, Howard Booksenbaum, and Michael Corr, (New York: Macmillan and Company, 1975).

[3]"Schlesinger's Czardom Takes Shape," TIME, March 7, 1977, 57.

[4]"The Battle of the Barrels Begins," TIME, January 3, 1977, 69.

[5]Ibid., 70.

[6]"Oil Consuming Countries to Draw Closer," The Oil and Gas Journal, July 24, 1972, 8.

[7]Allen H. Hammond, William D. Metz and Thomas H. Haugh II, Energy and the Future, (Boston: American Association for the Advancement of Science, 1973), 64.

[8]"World Energy: Decision That Must Be Taken Soon," Financial Times, August 3, 1973, 3.

[9]Ibid., 4.

[10]James E. Akins, "The Oil Crisis: This Time The Wolf is Here," Foreign Affairs, Volume 51,

No. 3, April 1973, 475.

[11]"Oil Buyers Beginning to Cut Purchases From OPEC States Raising Prices 10%," The Wall Street Journal, January 6, 1977, 3.

[12]A comprehensive, well-organized analysis of domestic energy sources and priorities is contained in Our Energy Future: The Role of Research, Development and Demonstration in Reaching a National Consensus on Energy Supply, by Don E. Kash, Michael D. Devine, and others, (Norman: University of Oklahoma Press, 1976).

[13]Barry Commoner, Howard Booksenbaum and Michael Corr, editors, Energy and Human Welfare, Volume II, (New York: Macmillan and Company, 1975), 91.

[14]James Boyd, Alvin M. Weinberg and Dennis L. Meadows, "Resources and Economic Growth, The American Future: A Dialogue," The Wilson Quarterly, Volume I, No. 1, Autumn 1976.

[15]Donald Rice, "Shortages and Economic Planning," The Wall Street Journal, March 14, 1977, 16.

[16]"Two-Tier Pricing Hasn't Weakened OPEC, Western Energy Group Aide Says," The Wall Street Journal, December 22, 1976, 1.

[17]Muhammad S. Al-Mahdi, The Pricing of Crude Oil in the International Market: A Search for Equitable Criteria," a paper presented at the Eighth Arab Petroleum Congress, Algiers, May-June, 1972.

[18]The politics of oil, energy policy and planning, and the public interest are documented in depth in Robert Engler's The Brotherhood of Oil and Kenneth W. Dam's Oil Resources: Who Gets What How? both published by the University of Chicago Press, Chicago, 1976.

[19]These marches were originally planned to support allocation demands; instead, the marchers protested in favor of price control regulations.

[20]Ray Vicker, "Push for Petroleum," The Wall Street Journal, March 8, 1977, 1. A Challenge to conventional wisdom on the energy crisis as it affects Americans, fuel shortages and over-consumption, and seesawing policy of the United States government in the energy market is thoroughly documented in Perspectives on U.S. Energy Policy: A Critique of Regulation, edited by Edward J. Mitchell, (New York: Praeger Special Studies, 1976).

[21]Richard F. Janssen, "Economic Shock Wave From Oil Price Rises in '73 Still Hurts West," The Wall Street Journal, March 10, 1977, 26.

[22]"High Hurdles for Imports," TIME, March 14, 1977, 46.

[23]Gottfried Haberler, Oil Inflation, Recession And The International Monetary System, (Washington, D. C.: American Enterprise Institute, 1976), Reprint No. 45, 179.

[24]Jahangir Amuzegar, "OPEC and The Dollar Dilemma," Foreign Affairs, July 1978, Volume 56, No. 4, 740-745.

[25]Ibid., 749.

CHAPTER VI

THE JAPANESE EXPERIENCE:
A MIRACLE OF FREE ENTERPRISE

Since World War II Japan has emerged as the world's third largest industrial country. This phenomenal economic growth, over a relatively limited span of time, is unprecendented in the history of industrialization. It appears to be a direct result of the persistence of capitalism's political economic organization in all economies striving for an advantageous position in the global marketplace. Japan has also distinguished itself in industrial trade by shifting its emphasis from being mainly a provider of labor-intensive products, such as textiles, pottery and Christmas tree ornaments, to being the leading world exporter of steel, ships, optical equipment, and consumer electronics. It is also a leading contender in heavy machinery and sophisticated business machines and, accordingly, has strengthened its international balance of payments position to the level of debtor nation with the status of lender to other countries.[1]

In order to understand Japan's impressive performance it is important to recognize that economic behavior, incentives, and performance are shaped by legal structures and other institutional arrangements, by the political system, government policy goals and means of implementation, and finally by individual and societal values and ideologies. Japan is a business oriented society. Its domestic environment has, for the most part, supported a free enterprise economic system. Since 1955 the conservative, pro-business, pro-agriculture Liberal Democratic party has promoted political stability. The country's economic policy has been effectively administered by the able, purposeful, highly motivated, elite bureaucracy of central government. Japan was never more market-oriented than in the 1960's when success based on free, private enterprise came to be broadly accepted as a goal.[2]

Many westerners who are not particularly
well acquainted with Japanese history believe the
emperors themselves were responsible for the nation's industrialization. They point to the
Meiji Constitution as evidence that the emperor
was by conviction democratic. In reality his
role in these events is hard to determine since
Meiji was only a fifteen year old boy possessed
of little business acumen when he became emperor
in 1967. Under Meiji's father, Emperor Komei,
the foundation of power in Japan was beginning to
shift from the shogunate to the imperial court.
With the accession of the new emperor the pro-
vincial daimyo joined the court nobles and over-
threw the shogunate. This restoration of imperial political power led to the building of a
Westernized industrial nation. According to
Jean Lequiller this momentous shift in power was
accomplished by only a score of men, using what
Roy Miller, in his book The Japanese Language,
called the newly discovered charismatic powers of
the emperor.[3] Everything was done in his name.
As the years passed Emperor Meiji played an ever
more active role in the political and decision
making activities of Japan. Since he was in
reality the charismatic power behind the actual
rulers almost anything could be accomplished in
his name as the legitimizing authority. And,
much was, including the astonishing development
of the nation's industrial complex. This was
done by imaginative men who sparked industrialization by borrowing technology from other countries in order to effect similar speedy results.
In Japan this propensity to borrow was quite
high. In fact Daniel L. Spencer has written that
"Japan has an existing accumulated stock of technical knowledge which antedated Western contact
and enabled them to absorb foreign high-level
technology."[4] Although Mr. Spencer addressed
himself to contemporary, postwar Japan, his com-
ments apply equally well to the Meiji period
which brought industrialization to dramatic
fruition.[5]

Japan rarely seems to have made any important changes until faced by seeming calamities.

A major example of this phenomenon, which contributed to the miracle of contemporary Japan, is
the nation's status in naval affairs and new ter-
ritories acquired as a result of the Portsmouth
Treaty which brought the Russo-Japanese war to an
end in 1905. Another example is Japan's entry
into commerce with the West as a result of Com-
modore Perry's naval expeditions to that country
in the early 1800's. In whatever spheres Japan
seemed to lag behind China it took that country
as its model in the arts, the sciences, craftwork
and agriculture.[6] Then power fell into the hands
of militarily adventurous men who, as a result of
declaring war on the United States on December 7,
1941, almost brought the country to utter destruction. Despite continued opposition by large
segments of the army, however, the government
finally surrendered. The occupation which followed was unbelievably benevolent. Hundreds of
millions of dollars were given to the conquered
country; the occupation forces provided technology and facilities for the revivication of the
economy.

By 1960, however, the government came to
recognize that rapid economic growth solved a
multitude of problems. In 1961 the ten-year in-
come-doubling plan epitomized the era of what was
viewed as virtuous growth. This was a long-range
projection for industrial growth reflecting a
doubling within ten years of individual incomes.
Its result was the creation of good jobs and the
regeneration of declining industries. In addition, and very importantly, it enhanced Japan's
power and prestige.[7] Some observers have cre-
dited industrial tycoons like Matsushita, Honda
and Sazo Idemitsu for Japan's present day status.[8] Others have cynically noted that under the
shadow of the United States all of Japan's energies have gone into getting rich, a process made
easier by not having to spend anything on defense.[9] Whatever the basic reasons for Japan's
phenomenal growth, we must recognize that it has
executed radical changes of course, very often
taking nations completely by surprise. Its
nature, basically, is the human parallel of the
country's geological situation; an apparently

solid structure subject to violent earthquakes. Whatever may be developing, however, in the political consciousness of Japan, the physical reality of its growing industrial wealth and the strong desire for material comfort and stability must naturally be an incentive to avoid drastic changes.

How has Japan used modern technology to economic advantage and what organizational obstacles to industrial growth has it encountered? While Japanese economic development has emulated the Capitalist model it has seemingly pursued very little of the spirit of Capitalism.[10] Instead, a marked and persistent aspect of postwar Japan has been the high priority given to economic growth. The loss of World War II with all its destruction initially caused the Japanese government to focus its priorities and efforts on economic reconstruction and the political, social, and economic reforms of the Allied occupation aimed at establishing a democratic Japan generated a new vitality and a widespread sense of participation.[11] Attention to the solution of individual inequities and the provision of public services was deferred.

Mr. Soichiro Honda, the famed motorcycle manufacturer, attributed the nation's phenomenal economic recovery to the fact that Japan lost the war. He said: "We have done well out of losing. With everything flattened, we could start from scratch, plan from the word go and think big."[12] The Korean War, which erupted during a deep depression in Japan, provided the stimulus for the economic boom of 1956-57. Later, during the 1963-65 recession, at the height of the Vietnamese War, the economy was again stimulated. In both instances United States procurement and expenditures for these wars were the saving grace.[13]

The banks also played a vital role in Japanese economic development. When the rulers of Meiji Japan decided to 'Westernize' in order to build an industrial society that could achieve

economically what it could not accomplish militarily, they found it necessary to provide for
the means to accumulate capital and to create or-
gans for trade transaction and finance. At the
time there were no banks in Japan; nor was there
a banking system. The closest thing were exchange houses; however, these knew nothing of
modern international or domestic banking. Therefore in 1872 the government set about creating a
banking system modeled on the British and the
American systems. It enacted National Bank Regulations and in 1873 founded the First National
Bank of Tokyo.[14]

Before the Bank of Japan was created in
1882, 143 national banks had been chartered. By
1893 Bank Regulations were enforced and already
there were 545 commercial banks in existence. At
first there were many bankruptcies but, with time
and experience these dwindled. Furthermore banking was made easier by government orders, in-
struction and guidance. It appears the bankers
did not consider themselves individual bankers
out to make a profit, rather they seemed to consider themselves semi-governmental bureaucrats.
Most of bank capital was provided by the government; sizeable blocks of shares were held by
Mitsui, Yasuda, Sumitomo and other Zaibatsu families thus giving Japan's economy a patriarchal
tone or emphasis. This state of affairs continued up to the end of World War II.[15] As demands
for funds and banking services proliferated Japanese bankers became entrepreneurs. They involved themselves deeply in industrial enterprises through both loans and ownership. The
tendency to interlocking directorates as opposed
to business individualism, seemed to the Japanese to be the best way for them to learn business and finance. It also appeared to be the
best way to build a tightly knit industrial -
structure and thus enable the economic growth of
the country.[16] Japanese banks and bankers, of
necessity closely allied to and controlled by
the central bank and the government, impose both
direct and indirect controls on industry. Of the
706 leading enterprises listed on the Tokyo Stock
Exchange, Japanese banks are frequently the major

individual shareholders. Thus they have an important voice in corporate decisions. Since the banks are, in turn, controlled by law by the Bank of Japan and the Ministry of Finance, many pressures can and are brought to bear on enterprise by government.[17] Currently the key actors in the complex net of Japanese enterprise relationships are the Ministry of Finance (MOF), the Ministry of International Trade and Industry (MITI),the prime minister's office, the cabinet, the Diet, Keindanren (the Federation of Economic Organizations), trade sector organizations, union leaders and company management.

Generally speaking, a Japanese enterprise is one entity of many interlocking connected entities. These are all interrelated in a variety of ways. Top managers in most of these groupings of companies belong to their own club; a sort of overall board of directors. They meet regularly, discuss business matters affecting the group, and formulate strategies. While in the United States such alliances would constitute collusion or restraint of trade, in Japan there are no such concerns. This is common practice and through these alliances the aims of the industrial company are subordinated to the aims of the group.

In the case of joint ventures with foreign companies, or where marketing and sales agreements are executed, the government tries to importune the foreign partner in writing to conform to existing Japanese business customs and practices.[18] Harmony is the keynote and it must not be disrupted since it is the accepted corporate philosophy of Japanese free enterprise. This often causes problems because, in their transactions with individual Japnese businesses, foreign businessmen sometimes discover belatedly that the companies with which they are dealing have a status, duties and obligations to a major industrial group or to some of its family members and that, before any important decision is made, its effect upon other members of the group are carefully considered. As a result, foreigners frequently complain that after

TABLE 6

DISTRIBUTION OF OWNERSHIP/ASSETS OF JAPAN'S LARGE CORPORATIONS, BY GROUP AFFILIATION, 1955, 1962 and 1970[a]

AFFILIATE GROUP	Percent Ownership/Asset Distribution		
	1955	1962	1970
State Enterprise Groups[b]	62.2%	50.1%	38.3%
Long-term Credit Bank Groups[c]	2.1	3.3	4.3
Private Financial Institution Groups[d]	23.3	28.4	29.2
Giant Industrial Corporations[e]	5.6	9.5	8.8
Foreign-owned Enterprises	1.0	1.4	1.4
Companies Outside the Affiliate System	5.8	7.3	18.0
	100.0%	100.0%	100.0%

Sources: Y. Miyazaki, Sengo Nihon No keizai kiko (Economic Organization of Postwar Japan),(Shinh-yoronsha, 1966), p. 208; and idem, "Showa 40 nendo kigyo shudan hyo ni tsuite" (On Corporate group tabulations in 1965), in shigeto tauru (ed.), Atarashu seiji keizaigaku o motomete III (For a New Political Economics III), (Keiso Shobo, 1970), Table 2, p. 381.
   a. Large corporations defined as those with tangible assets of more than five billion yen.
   b. Public corporations whose capital is wholly or partly government owned.
   c. Affiliates of long-term credit banks whose capital is partly government owned.

TABLE 6 (Continued)

d. Affiliates of zaibatsu and large banks.
   These are controlled by law, by the
   Bank of Japan and the Ministry of Finance.
e. Corporations with vertical and conglom-
   erate structures of subsidiaries and
   affiliates.

NOTE: It should be noted, in reviewing these
distributions, that the public sector's (State
Enterprise Groups) predominance makes it bulk
large in the total. Nevertheless, though its
share is dropping, much of its control is still
exercised through the Private Financial Institution Groups in the form of Bank of Japan and
Ministry of Finance legal control. Independent
private corporations outside the affiliate system have expanded the most rapidly, although
each private sector group has picked up part of
the state enterprises' declining share.

More recent figures are not available at
this time. Perhaps this is because, as Mr. Ezra
F. Vogel, Chairman of Harvard University's Council on East Asian Studies, so aptly expressed it
in the May-June 1978 issue of Harvard Business
Review, "the widely held notion of 'Japan, Inc.'
is exaggerated." He added that "there is no
monolithic business-government link." He further
said that "even so, the cooperation (without in-
corporation) between the large combines and the
government bureaucracy is impressive in its
strength and focus on the common economic good--
especially in view of its achievements world-
wide."

TABLE 7

IMPACT OF IMPORT MARKET SHARE LOSS ON 1977 IMPORTS TO JAPAN FROM THE UNITED STATES

Category	Total 1977 Japan Imports (billion $)	1968-70 U.S. Share (percent)	1976-77 U.S. Share (percent)	Impact of Share Loss (million $)
Food	$11.3	37.8%	33.5%	$ 485
Wood Fiber, Rubber, etc.	6.5	29.6	31.4	(117)
Metal Ores and Scrap	4.8	14.8	5.0	470
Coal	3.5	58.0	32.2	901
Refined Petroleum Products	2.2	21.2	7.0	310
Cotton and Wool	2.0	11.0	17.0	(120)
Basic Materials Sub-Total	$30.3			$1,930
Capital Equipment	$ 4.4	61.0%	51.3%	$ 428
Chemicals	2.9	41.2	39.6	46
Finished Metals	2.0	8.6	6.3	46
Consumer Nondurables	1.5	32.4	12.6	296
Consumer Durables	1.3	39.5	27.2	161
Textiles	0.7	8.7	5.6	22
Manufactured Sub-Total	$12.8			$ 999
Total of Categories Listed	$43.1		Total Impact	$2,929

NOTE: All Japanese imports are calculated on a customs clearance basis. The categories included in this table represent 94 percent of Japan's total imports in 1977, excepting crude petroleum.
SOURCE: James C. Abegglen and Thomas M. Hout, "Facing Up To The Trade Gap With Japan," Foreign Affairs, Fall 1978, Volume 57, No. 1, 148.

negotiating with Japanese businessmen, for however short or long a time, they had believed an agreement final and it was not at all so. Perhaps a last-minute change was introduced, or perhaps nothing may have happened after the final agreement. And sometimes, even after contracts have actually been signed, nothing has been done to implement them.[19] The reason may never be explained very likely because somewhere within the Japanese group relationships or in dealings with the bankers or bureaucracy some opposition was injected. What to a Westerner is a very simple decision may not be at all simple in Japan. Thus, the contemporary Japanese structure, while it may be modern, is based on ancient feudal tradition that is at variance with Western logic.[20] Everyone, from the Minister of Finance on down has a place in the structure that is his so long as he obeys and conforms to the rules.

We have already noted a close connection between business and the Japanese government and, as well, the close resemblance between governmental bureaucrats and industrial managers. The Japanese government, like all governments, is a collection of bureaucrats topped by politicians. Like all other bureaucracies that of the Japanese performs in the light of inherited customs, traditions, attitudes, practices and prejudices.[21] The top Japanese bureaucrats, like the top managers in industry are mostly Meiji men, trained and educated by older, early Meiji men. Thus, in government as in industry, one must await the rise to power of the new youth before a break from feudal tradition is effected. As a British report puts it: "The very intimate and manifold connection at all levels between government and industry are an important factor in the attitudes and policies of both.[22] These relationships are reputed to be of a strength and effectiveness unequaled in any other industrialized capitalist state.

Contributing substantially to this phenomenon are the so-called public corporations. Marshall E. Dimock, educator and political scientist, writes: "I have seen estimates that as much as forty percent of all the nation's economic activity is controlled by government enterprise."[23] Professor Dimock estimates that over a million people are employed by public corporations, and his study of the subject is based on 108 such corporations, but, as he points out, that figure "does not include all corporate enterprises that might be listed in the public or semi-public sector, but only those that the government recognizes as its proper official concern."[24] As already noted, the Ministry of Finance exercises control over industry through the Bank of Japan and city banks' administrative guidance, however, is usually given by the Ministry of International Trade and Industry. What the Japanese call window guidance is made use of, as well, by other ministries which under its guise impose on occasion extremely stringent controls.

We find, therefore, that under the Japanese political system we have elements of the United States' regulatory bodies and powers, nationalization of industry as in Great Britain and, substantively, a mixed economy. Under this system Japan has thrived; it has performed what has been referred to as an industrial miracle.[25]

It should be noted however, that in 1975 the economy of Japan was declining so Japanese businessmen began a concentrated effort to capture a large part of the American market for Japanese exports. The most dramatic manifestation of this crisis was the accumulation, by the end of 1977, of a U.S. trade deficit with Japan of eight billion dollars. By 1978 year's end the trade imbalance between the two nations had reached a staggering $13 billion.

As a key element in the overall United States balance-of-payments deficit, a recurring irritant in United States-Japanese overall relations, and a significant factor in the decline of the dollar, trade relations between the

United States and Japan are now a critically
important problem.

As the deficit grows, so does, for many,
discomfort with the now tenuous explanation of
Japanese surplus. Japan did indeed achieve no-
toriety by promoting exports and restricting
imports. But for some time it has been doing
less promoting and restricting, yet watching
its surplus embarrassingly grow. Further, to
perceive the problem in these terms tends to
emphasize the role of governments on both sides.

Yet, it is increasingly clear that the market mechanism, not distortions of it, is the
main driving force in bilateral trade. This
brings us to the United States. Frightened
American businessmen have been accusing the
Japanese of almost everything from outright
cheating to simply working too hard.[26] Conced-
ing their own ideological opposition to interference in free enterprise, they are nevertheless begging the United States government for
help for the sake of survival. Thus the American government faces a classic dilemma; should
it protect beleaguered industries threatened
with extinction at the hands of their Japanese
competition, or can it somehow persuade "Japan,
Inc.," (the term often used to describe Japan's
postwar industrial colossus), to let up, in the
long-range interest of overall harmony? Before
taking this important step, however, consideration should be given to the fact that most
American companies that are begging for government assistance have really never made a serious
effort to exploit world markets in a carefully
thought-out fashion. Perhaps, they should do
so before asking for government aid. As a
matter of fact United States producers can and
should try to contain the Japanese in the marketplace. Exacerbating the issue, moreover, is
Japan's own dilemma, an economic bind born of
the worldwide energy crisis, that drives Japanese firms to increase exports in a desperate
bid to compensate for sluggish conditions at
home.[27]

These jolting economic and political setbacks, which include the Lockheed payoff scan-
dal, appear economically disastrous. As a result, the Japanese are threatening to turn a-
way from the conservative politicians who have
ruled in close partnership with businessmen for
more than two prosperous decades. This should
not be surprising since it is in the national
character for the Japanese to execute drastic
changes of course in the face of adversity.
Japan, in fact, is adapting to difficult problems with remarkable grace.[28]

Both managers and workers have come out of
their recent adversity with more verve than
ever. The tradition of life-time employment
largely survived two years of recession, pre-
venting widespread layoffs and making the Japanese even more dedicated to their jobs. In a
Tokyo bank lobby, painters readily work throughout the night to avoid interfering with business. Employees at Toyota's frantically busy
plants near Nagoya suggest vital ways to shave
production costs, right down to such small
things as substituting newspapers for expensive
vinyl as wrappings for hubcaps delivered to the
assembly line. Matsushita Electric's factory
workers, who voluntarily helped retailers sell
off swollen inventories during the recession,
are willingly accepting increased automation to
bolster the company's rebound. Takeshi Asozu,
Matsushita's labor-relations director, observes:
"Employees realize how important this is for
business---and for their own good."

For their part, top executives are acting
to regain the old impetus. They are working
overtime under the guidance of the influential
MITI to find new ways to raise efficiency, devise new products, and broaden markets. But
the reassuring rituals of an older Japan are
carefully preserved. A chief executive will
still take the time to see a departing visitor
to the elevator, where the customary bows are
calmly exchanged. And businessmen still spend
more money entertaining clients and colleagues

(about $6.4 billion in 1976) than the nation
puts into defense. Business is picking up
rapidly in both international and domestic markets. Currently exports of autos, color tele-
vision sets, computers and entire industrial
plants are setting records. At home, renewed
consumer confidence is filling department
stores with so many customers on weekends that
just getting through the doors is difficult.
The gathering rush of business activity may
well enlarge the annual gross national product.[29]

While the economy is gradually being re-
structured, a similar transformation is taking
place in politics. The stunning revelations of
high-level corruption almost certainly will
erode the exclusive control of government by
the coalition of conservatives known as the
Liberal Democrats. But the present crisis is
not radicalizing the Japanese, who are innately
conservative; instead, it promises to modernize
their almost feudal system. That, at least, is
the expectation of many thoughtful Japanese.
Says Jiro Tokuyama, managing director of Nomura
Research Institute, a subsidiary of the nation's
largest securities company: "Just as America re-
gained confidence after Vietnam and Watergate,
I think we'll do so after cleaning up the political garbage that has piled up." The very
fact that former Prime Minister Kakuei Tanaka
was arrested and charged with taking Lockheed
money certainly indicates the vitality of Japanese democracy.[30]

The modernization process probably will
take several years, however, because the political system itself is seriously flawed. The
ruling party is a loose collection of nine factions, most of which are headed by elderly men
who respond sluggishly to public opinion. As
Japan grapples with the challenge of both align-
ing its economy and reshaping its political system, it will undoubtedly face many nervous mo-
ments and its share of failure. But it has always managed to make the best of misfortunes in

the past. Its lack of domestic raw materials led to the development of bulk carriers, advanced shipbuilding techniques, and efficient factories on tidewater sites; converting a resource-poor nation into a powerful international competitor. Now the higher costs of energy and raw materials and the Japanese government are stimulating changes of equal promise. The goal is, of course, to prevent economic recovery from going into relapse. This latest stimulus is taking the form of increased public works spending, housing loans and other measures aimed at keeping the economy on track toward an assured seven percent growth in 1979.[31]

While political risks are inherently difficult to weigh, the outlook for Japan, as a competitive power in the emerging global economic system, appears good because the nation's political climate allows capitalism to flourish. Japan's economic stability, furthermore, permits it to go about modernizing the whole society without completely wrecking its unifying traditions. Yet, to assure further economic growth this highly industrialized country is now likely to need the Third World to sustain effective demand for its expanding production.[32] Though poor nations have not previously been important in the economic calculations of the rich nations, Japan and in fact the whole of the developed world, must recognize that they cannot be sustained with the continued improverishment of the Third World.

[1] Eugene J. Kaplan, "Japan's Foreign Trade-
-The Perils of Success" United States/Japan
Trade Council Report from the Special National
Foreign Convention issue of the American Banker,
November 15, 1976. The United States/Japan
Trade Council has noted that, from 1965 to 1970,
Japan actually doubled its economic investment
in industry.

[2] Johannes Hirschmeier and Tsumehiko Yui,
The Development of Japanese Business, 1600-1973,
(Cambridge, Massachusetts: Harvard University
Press, 1975), 192.

[3] Ibid., 303.

[4] Daniel L. Spencer, "An External Military
Presence, Technological Transfer and Structural
Change," Kyklos, XVIII (1965), facs. 3, 10.

[5] James Morley, Dilemmas of Growth in Prewar
Japan, (Princeton: Princeton University Press,
1974), 68.

[6] "Which Way Will The Japanese Economy Go?"
United States/Japan Trade Council. Washington,
D. C., 1976, 5.

[7] Jean Lequiller, Japanese History of the
Twentieth Century, (Japan, Paris: Editions Sirly,
1966), 81.

[8] Marshall E. Dimock, The Japanese Technocracy, (New York and Tokyo: Walker/Westerhill
Publishing, 1968), 51.

[9] T. F. M. Adams and N. Kobavashi, The World
of Japanese Business, (Tokyo: Kodansha International, Ltd., 1969), 92.

[10] Ibid., 98.

[11]Johannes Hirschmeier and Tsumehiko Yui, The Development of Japanese Business, 1600-1973, (Cambridge, Massachusetts: Harvard University Press, 1975), 198.

[12]Ibid., 210.

[13]Donald Kirk, "The High Cost of Doing Business With Japan," Saturday Review, March 19, 1977, 21. A 1975 study of Japanese business and marketing techniques is contained in M. Y. Yoshimo's Marketing in Japan, sponsored by the Center for International Business at Pepperdine University, (Los Angeles: University of California).

[14]Edward F. Denison and William K. Chung, How Japan's Economy Grew So Fast, The Sources of Postwar Expansion, (Washington, D. C.: The Brookings Institution, 1976), 105.

[15]Ibid., 216.

[16]Inazo Nitobe, Western Influence in Modern Japan, (Chicago: University of Chicago Press, 1931), 48.

[17]Hugh Patrick and Henry Rosovsky, Asia's New Giant: How The Japanese Economy Works, (Washington, D. C.: The Brookings Institution, 1976), 134. Another 1976 Brookings study, by I. M. Destler, Priscilla Clapp, Hideo Sato and Haruhiko Fukui, Managing an Alliance: The Politics of U. S.-Japanese Relations, provides excellent background material on the impact of politics, both American and Japanese, on the economy of Japan.

[18]A Typical clause that Japanese authorities like to insert in foreign joint venture agreements is: "The (joint venture) new company shall be managed with full consideration of the commercial and management customs of Japan."

[19]T.K.M. Adams and N. Kobayashi, The World of Japanese Business, (Tokyo: Kodansha International, Ltd., 1969), 60.

[20]Ibid., 81.

[21]W. G. Beasley, The Modern History of Japan, (New York: Praeger Publishing, 1970 and rev. 1974), 71.

[22]"Report to the Federation of British Industries," Consider Japan, op.cit.

[23]Marshall E. Dimock, The Japanese Technocracy, (New York: and Tokyo: Walker/Westherhill Publishing, 1968), 82.

[24]Ibid., 86.

[25]Edwin O. Reischauer, "The Postwar Miracle," The Wilson Quarterly, Volume 1, Number 4, Summer 1977, 56.

[26]"Marketing in Japan Takes Twisty Turns, Foreign Firms Find," The Wall Street Journal, March 9, 1977, 1.

[27]Donald Kirk, "The High Cost of Doing Business With Japan," Saturday Review, March 19, 1977, 25.

[28]Ruth Benedict, The Chrysanthemum and the Sword, (Boston: Houghton Mifflin Company, 1946). This work examines closely the pattern of Japanese culture.

[29]Louise Kraar, "Adversity Is Helping the Japanese Refashion Their Future," FORTUNE, October 1976, 127.

[30]Ibid., 129.

[31]Mike Tharp, "Japan Unveils New Stimulative Package In Bid For Goal of 7% Economic Growth," The Wall Street Journal, September 5, 1978, 6.

[32]Peter Berger, "A Hard-Line View of Inequality Among Nations," FORTUNE, May 1977, 139.

CHAPTER VII

THIRD WORLD DEVELOPMENT:
THE CHINESE INITIATIVE

We have noted substantial differences among developed nations, and these consist of behavioral transformations linked to their political and social histories. Each nation is, after all, a product of its own unique historical experience. We have now come a long way from the libertarian thinking of John Stewart Mill, one of those men of vision who were responsible for the spirit of Fabianism. Mill, in writing of the limits to the authority of society over the individual, commented on the existence of diverse responses of nations to the stimuli of industry and trade. Since then studies of development have proliferated and a mass of knowledge of fundamental similarities and differences among nations has been accumulated. Economists now recognize the complexity of economic development and the wide variety of responses that have been made by nations faced, each in its own history and circumstances, with the challenges of economic change.[1]

How far is the economic theory of the industrially advanced free market nations applicable to the developing Third World countries? A British Labor Government minister, Shirley Williams, addressed herself to this question when she spoke about the moral obligation of the West to bring about a global redistribution of resources. According to Williams and others who share her Fabian Socialist view, individuals have a right to a guaranteed minimal standard of living which it is the duty of government to supply through redistribution of the national income. Mrs. Williams appears to feel that nations too have economic rights it is the duty of the world community to recognize. This doctrine was formally adopted by the United Nations General Assembly in 1974 in a Declaration on Economic Rights and Duties. Nevertheless, some economists argue that such generalizations of economic

103

theory are based on the particular circumstances of the advanced countries and are, therefore not universally valid.[2] They argue that Western economic theory is geared to the preoccupations of the advanced countries which, having already achieved sustained economic growth (supposedly, in the case of the Third World, through colonialism and capitalist exploitation) are concerned with other problems, such as optimum allocation of resources, the maintenance of full employment, and perhaps the prevention of ultimate stagnation. Thus conventional economic theory is largely irrelevant for the central problems of the underdeveloped countries.

Meanwhile, critics vary widely in the emphasis and priorities they attach to solutions but they share a common viewpoint relative to their attack on the applicability of economic theory, free trade and laissez-faire politics to the underdeveloped countries.[3] Thus their sharpest attack on Western economic theory is reserved for the laissez-faire approach rather than for the post-Keynesian economics used in support of deficit financing for economic development. In the early days of Third World development the case for deficit financing was argued mainly on the basis that the investment expenditure financed by pure creation would expand the money incomes and would, theoretically, keep them stabilized at a planned level. It was expected that the result would be an increase in output which would then catch up to the stabilized income level and destroy the consequent inflation.[4]

All this represents a bad start for economic development of the Third World. The chances for industrialization and the development of a free enterprise economy in the immediate future are distinctly slim. Perhaps it would be wise for underdeveloped nations, regardless of their ambitions, to emulate China which, by contrast, recognized long ago that agriculture should be emphasized. It seems that the nation's efforts

in this direction have borne fruit. According
to western estimates of agriculture output,
productivity increased by about 30 percent in
this sector between 1953-57 and 1968-72. If
this fact has important political implications
for the present and the future, it also has
positive implications on the purely economic
plane in that it demonstrates effectively that
agricultural development is not impossible
within the framework of the conditions pre-
vailing in the less-developed countries of
Asia, i.e., great population growth coupled
with a limited quantity of land whose fertility
is mediocre and climatic conditions are mostly
unfavorable.[5] It is theoretically conceivable
that agriculture development in such circumstances would be impossible. The regression in
agriculture productivity suffered by countries
in Africa and Asia suggest, furthermore, that
it has been so. Nevertheless, we must remember
that China, by comparison with other larger
Asian countries, has more agricultural land
available and that she was not plagued by
colonialism.

China's success and the, at least partial,
failure of the non-communist Third World pose
the question as to what are the causes under-
lying the difference. Unfortunately there are
no clear cut answers to this question, since
if, to simplify the matter, we take the two
great Asian powers, China and India, we have to
admit that before 1949, while their levels of
economic development were fairly similar, their
structural conditions were much less so.[6] In
addition to differences in agriculture which
have already been taken into consideration
(availability of land and the existence of a
plantation economy) we also have to admit that
the absence of a direct long-established colonial regime in China must have influenced the industrial sector; English manufactures had pene-
trated the country sufficiently to cause the
handicrafts of India other than those engaged
in art products largely to disappear, whereas
they continue to exist in China and played

their part in the process of industrialization
But the fact that India received more financial
aid than China must also be considered.[7]

It would appear, then, that the overall
rate of growth for Third World economy will be
determined by the rate of growth of its slowest
moving sector, agriculture. The stimulation of
that sector's output, therefore, requires the
diversion of a considerable part of the resources of the manufacturing sector from capital
goods to consumer goods. This would, of
course, slow down the rate of growth. On the
other hand, however, attempts to use negative
pressures such as taxation or compulsory collection of produce may also lead to a peasants'
strike, resulting in a lesser amount of agricultural surplus.[8] In this situation, many
economists again have toyed with the idea of
accelerating economic growth by deficit financing to facilitate the transfer of disguised
unemployment from agriculture into productive
work, particularly in the construction of irri-
gation projects or roads. They also argue that
this type of financing may be pursued without
serious long-term consequences because the com-
pletion of the capital projects will add to the
output of agriculture and other consumers'
goods. This is altogether different from saying
that the social cost of making use of the disguised unemployment is zero. On the contrary,
it is recognized that there is a genuine social
cost in doing so in the form of extra consumption by the workers on the capital projects. In
fact, deficit financing appears to be called for
because this extra consumption cannot be met out
of taxation and voluntary savings, so that
forced saving has to be imposed through inflation. So while Third World consumer prices
must, consequently, go up, the degree that this
inflation will be self-destroying will depend
on how far the wage earners in the underdeveloped countries will go on saving and spending in
stable proportions in the face of rising prices
of consumers' goods.[9]

A main justification, then, for deficit

finance in less developed countries, as in any
other country, must be the existence of unemployed resources due to deficient demand. If
resources are unemployed or under-utilized,
real output and real savings can be increased
by governments running budget deficits financed
either by printing money or issuing government
bonds to the banking system and the public.
Although deficit finance is likely to be inflationary in the short run, there is an important
analytical distinction between the means by
which additional resources are made available
for investment through deficit finance and the
means by which savings are generated by inflation.[10] In the former case savings are generated from the increase in real output; in the
latter case, by a reduction in real consumption
which may result from a combination of three
factors; money illusion, the inability to maintain real expenditure, and income redistribution.

Current actions and rhetoric of the developing nations, however, herald an era of demands that threatens to diminish the living
standards and political influence of the industrialized world. The nations, furthermore, in
their quest for their own progress, present a
challenge to the rest of the world to demon-
strate that the international structure can
give them a role, a fair share, dignity and responsibility.[11]

It appears that the rich nations, then,
must place such demands of the Third World in
their proper historical perspective, agree on a
strategy of serious negotiations, help crystal-
lize certain negotiating areas and principles,
and determine the negotiating forums where mutu-
ally beneficial agreements can be thrashed out.
It is in this spirit that the international community must move quickly to develop a negotiating strategy with a view to developing a Third
World free market economy in order that the affected nations may fulfill their aspirations.
Narrowing down the area of negotiation to man-

ageable proportions, however, and selecting
priorities fairly carefully so that dialogue
can move from the least divisive issues to the
more difficult ones becomes a step-by-step
approach. Conferences can seldom produce decisions unless agreement has been reached
quietly in advance. At present, such quiet efforts are needed to reach preliminary under-
standings and a political consensus on the
nature and form of the negotiations between
the rich and poor nations. While detailed negotiations may have to proceed on a case-by-
case basis, negotiations of an overall umbrella
is absolutely essential if the advantage of
collective bargaining is to be retained.[12]

It is not the intent here to attempt to
prepare a concrete blueprint of a new planetary
bargain that the poor nations seem to be seeking at present, but rather merely to advance a
positive free market approach toward reaching
such a bargain. The report of the group of
experts on the structure of the United Nations
system is aimed at providing sensible negotiating forums within the United Nations framework for an orderly dialogue on the elements of
a New International Economic Order.[13] Techno-
cratic proposals are easy to formulate. But
what is really required for the success of the
deliberations between rich and poor nations is
political vision that is inspired by the promise of the future, not clouded by the contro-
versies of the past nor mired in the short run
problems of the present. Such strategies will
not, however, stem the inflationary spiral
whether or not there are unemployed resources.
Inflation is already out of hand and we have
recognized in our study of the nationalization
of British industry that the quantity of capital investment is not always its cure-all. In
fact the regard of investment as a good in itself, or of taking its productivity for granted,
leads to waste since it inhibits scrutiny of
investment programs and projects.[14]

Meanwhile, Third World countries are engaged in a struggle to attain a strong economic

foothold in the world marketplace. An example
of this effort was the nationalization in 1977
of foreign companies in Zaire. Unfortunately,
the Zaire government came to realize that the
taken-over industries were failing under domestic management. The foreign owners and
managers of the nationalized companies were
then invited to come back to save the industries that were previously taken from them. In
return they were promised sixty percent ownership of their former one hundred percent investment.

In contemplating the economic scene in the
Third World, it is important to remember that
the supply of capital and its likely productivity are closely related. People apt to use
capital productively will either generate it
themselves, or be able to find others who will
make it available to them on commercial terms.
The fact that so much of Third World industry
now relies on inter-governmental aid causes a
presumption that these funds will not be used
productively.[15] In many parts of the world,
South Asia, Africa, the Middle East and Ireland,
one can readily observe the phenomenon that
even where a very small amount of effort or
thought would maintain or improve the condition
of an asset the thought or effort is not forth-
coming. Yet in some of these countries huge
public investment programs are being undertaken
with extravagant assumptions about the return.

The insistence on the amount of investment
spending may also be an example of the naive
belief in the importance of the quantifiable
aspects of a situation, and of the related pre-
occupation with statistical end results.[16] Yet
the productivity of investment often depends on
many factors that cannot be readily quantified.
Moreover, even if the rate of investment in a
country is low, this by itself tells us little
about the situation unless we know it is low.
If we do not consider this, we are likely to
confuse symptom or effect with cause. For in-
stance, if investment is low because the politi-

cal climate, social conditions, or popular attitudes are uncongenial to private investment,
attempts to increase its volume will not by
themselves promote material progress, What is
needed are changes in the policies and attitudes that have caused it to be low.

Such policies and attitude changes are now
quite prevalent, as we have already noted, in
current debates concerning a new International
Economic Order. In the politically relevant
area of policy discussion two broad positions
may now be discerned. One tends toward accommodation with Third World demands for resource
distributions, the other toward resistance.[17]
Both positions involve an amalgam of empirical
perceptions and moral judgements. In other
words, soft-liners argue for accommodation on
grounds of both expediency and justice, while
hard-liners contest the argument on, apparently,
the same grounds.

In studying both positions it would appear
that we should not take either one at its face
value. There is no reason why Western countries
should feel guilty about their economic dealings
with the Third World. They are not responsible
for their poverty. On the contrary, Western
economic influence, both during and after the
colonial period appears to have been the main-
spring of economic development throughout the
Third World. Nor is there much substance to
most theories about excess profits extorted by
Western companies. The average rate of return
on Western investments in the Third World has
not been greater than in other areas. The argument that the West has stolen the Third
World's finite resources is also unconvincing,
since those resources were developed for the
first time by Western companies and acquired
economic value only in relation to Western
needs.[18]

Beyond that, it seems clearly absurd, furthermore, to expect standards of political behavior that prevail, if erratically, in Western

TABLE 8

ECONOMIC SYSTEMS AND KEY ECONOMIC INDICATORS FOR THE THIRD WORLD

	Approximate 1974 Population (000 omitted)	Average Per Capita Income (1974 $)	Average Per Capita GNP (1976 $)	Average Gross domestic investment as a /% of 1973 GNP	Average Physical Quality of Life Index (1976)
ASIA	1,241,305	$278	$1,913	18.9	47
YUGOSLAVIA	21,130	1,179	1,680	25.3	84
P.R. OF CHINA	786,440	170	410	n.a.	57
AFRICA	360,432	266	499	19.7	28
LATIN AMERICA	297,333	888	967	20.3	70
GRAND TOTAL	2,706,640	$ 319	$ 967	n.a.	60

SOURCES: World Bank Atlas estimates; Basic Economic Data Sheet (World Tables, Part I); Cooerpative Economic Data Tables (World Tables, Part II).

TABLE 8 (Continued)

Economic Systems include:

M-L/Marxism - Leninism, commonly known as Communism.
TWSoc/Third World Socialism is embraced by societies whose beliefs
    are rooted in Nationalism and Tribalism. They, largely
    because of their experience with colonialism, reject capita-
    lism as identifiable with imperialism and exploitation.
    Finally, these governments pursue policies aimed at de-
    creasing the role of private property in the economy and
    curbing investment by private foreign firms.
SocDem/Social Democratic systems are identified so when the party
    in power is the Social Democratic party. The Social Demo-
    crats are in power mostly in industrially advanced and
    politically democratic nations and are cautious in their
    efforts to change existing systems, for example, nationaliz-
    ing economies.
MixEc/These combine elements of free enterprise competition with
    state ownership or direction of key industries.
Capit/Comprises free-market economic-political systems; i.e.,
    capitalism.

112

industrial democracies to be applied in Third
World countries that enjoy neither the economic
base nor the social cohesion to practice them.
Developing nations, such as Zaire, have much
to learn from the experience of the developed;
the most important lesson being that the latter
have formulated theories and policies with reference to their own special conditions. But
imitation will prove disastrous, as is already
becoming evident, because it means misshaping
one's own framework to make it conform to the
realities and interests of others.[19]

A disturbing feature of almost two decades
of organized developmental efforts in many
countries of the Southern Hemisphere is the
emergence of serious contradictions in these
economies. These contradictions are undermining
the growth process. The Indian economy can be
used to illustrate this situation. That nation's national and per capita incomes have increased although at a slower rate than envisaged
in the Five-Year Plans. As well, however, there
has been an increase in the extent and intensity
of poverty. More than forty percent of the population is still living below the poverty line,
which is generally identified as being an annual
per capita income of Rs. 240 (about thirty-three
dollars) at 1960-61 prices in the urban sector,
and Rs. 180 (approximately twenty-four dollars)
in the rural sector. Official statements con-
firm the fact that economic inequalities have
increased, with the rich gorwing richer and the
poor feeling more deprived in a relative sense;
even though they may be slightly better off than
before. Although India has been commended for
the success of its green revolution, there nevertheless is a shortage of foodgrains despite a
doubling of foodgrain production between 1951
and 1971. Furthermore prices of agricultural
produce are rising sharply. At the same rate,
increasing inequality in rural areas is genera-
ting social discontent and unrest. In 1972, one
bad monsoon seemed to neutralize the benefits of
the green revolution and created near-famine conditions in large drought-affected regions.

In the industrialization sector India's
progress appears impressive, although it is
accompanied by increases in industrial unrest,
unemployment, underemployment, rising prices of
manufacturers, unused capacity, power shortages,
and monopolistic tendencies. The traditional
section of small-scale and cottage industries,
which not only utilizes available resources
and skills but also is more employment-genera-
ting per unit of invested capital, is in a
state of crisis despite government subsidies
and encouragement. The value of annual exports
has increased by two and a half times since
1961 and is now diversified in both composition
and direction. Nevertheless balance of payments
deficits continue and debt-servicing will soon
consume one third of the country's export earnings. Literacy has more than doubled yet seventy percent of the population remains illiter-
ate and more persons are in that category today than were twenty years ago. As regards
India's self-reliance, in the narrow balance
of payments sense of the term, it appears that
the donor countries rather than the Planning
Commission determine the degree of self reliance.[20]

Those who have come to the conclusion that
the West cannot be the world's policeman appear
still to believe that it has the magic solution
to Third World poverty. there, indeed, are solutions, but they must be painfully approached.
Their success will no doubt depend to a considerable degree on the Third World countries themselves. Prosperity has to be earned, just as
a well-balanced political order has to evolve.
The great engine of economic development and of
political freedom in the West was private enterprise. It may well be, therefore, that for
similar things to be achieved in the Third World
a free enterprise economic organization is the
necessary foundation. A good working organization could in fact be patterned after that of
existing successful economies such as the United
States, West Germany, and Japan, just to name a
few. Obviously, the results would of necessity

TABLE 9

MULTINATION COMPANY OUTPUT IN
WORLD TRADE

Billions of Dollars			
	1978	1988	1998
Market world GNP (approximately ½ U.S.)	2900	4800	8000
Output associated with U.S. investment abroad	450	950	2000
Output associated with foreign investment in the U.S.	200	425	900
Output associated with other investment outside the U.S.	300	600	1300
Total output from international investment	950	1975	4200
"Internationalized Production" as % of Market world GNP	33%	41%	53%

SOURCE: Paper presented in October 1971 by political scientist Karl P. Savant of the University of Pennsylvania. The years 1978, 1988 and 1998 are projections.

NOTE: 1. According to FORTUNE researchers (FORTUNE, August 14, 1978, pp. 108-111) the real G. N.P. growth rate of the global economy slipped to 4.3 percent in 1977 from five percent the year before. Japan continued to expand more rapidly than the world as a whole though nowhere as fast as in the sixties. The Third World, which includes some members of OPEC who are still classified as developing countries, increased 4.8 percent in real output. This robust increase is primarily attributable to the 8.8 percent growth achieved by the OPEC countries. Gross planetary product totaled close to eight trillion dollars in 1977 of which five trillion dollars was produced in the industrialized countries.
    2. The international economic letdown, sometimes called stagflation or even slumpflation, is a period of unusually sluggish growth and uncomfortably high rates of inflation.

TABLE 9 (Continued)

Since productivity growth is a major ingredient
of G.N.P. growth it appears that, because of its
continued decline labor-force projections seem
to bode slow growth ahead in the industrial
world. The rising tide of social-welfare expenditures suggests that many countries are more
concerned with redistribution rather than with
growth. It is encouraging to observe that major
industrial countries are rapidly adjusting to
high energy costs, using much less of it per
unit of output. According to Lawrence Klein,
head of the global forecasting unit at the University of Pennsylvania, world growth is expected to be very moderate through 1982.

be relatively slow in coming.21 Experience in the OPEC countries has already taught us that waste and mismanagement of technology added to a lack of planning and training are counterproductive. In fact experience appears to indicate that in some countries a free enterprise agrarian economy, geared to the global marketplace, might well be the solution to economic ills.

Nevertheless, after almost thirty years of deep animosity between the United States, the world's richest nation, and the People's Republic of China, the world's most populous nation, Communist China is now pragmatically and vigorously seeking to expand its economic relations with the United States, Japan and Western Europe in order to promote its $600 billion modernization plan (through 1985). This, then, is the Chinese initiative. Suddenly and dramatically, on December 15, 1978, America's President Jimmy Carter announced the normalization of relations with the People's Republic of China (PRC) and the recognition of Peking as its sole legal government. Co-incidentally he announced the termination of formal relations with the Republic of China on Taiwan. No longer would the United States recognize the Taiwan Nationalists as the legitimate government of all China. Yet, it would be naive to assume that the interests of these countries in the Asian-Pacific region are congruent.22

Supporters of normalization argue that it will promote greater trade and cultural ties with the PRC without affecting commercial and cultural relations with Taiwan. Trade in the global marketplace has thus become the high point on the agenda of Sino-American issues. Pronormalization advocates, in order to strengthen their claims, point to the fact that Chinese foreign trade has risen from approximately thirteen billion dollars in 1976 to nearly twenty billion dollars in 1978. In addition long-term agreements totaling twenty seven billion dollars are reported already to have been en-

117

tered into. Between now and 1985 technology imports are expected to rise to between forty and two hundred billion dollars. For a variety of political reasons economic relations between the United States and China will encounter some formidable but not insurmountable difficulties. For example there exists a need to resolve (1) the frozen assets issue, (2) the granting of most-favored-nation status to China, (3) the making of trade with that country eligible for Export-Import Bank credits and (4) the problem of transfer of advanced technology under the control mechanisms created in 1949 to prevent the export of Western technology that might enhance the military capability of Communist countries.[23]

A serious constraint on exports to China will be its limited ability to pay for them. Though the country's credit status is excellent some of the early euphoria is fading and, according to Seth Lipsky of the Asian Wall Street Journal, there is a growing concern in Hong Kong that "foreign banks and suppliers are offering (and Peking might inadvertently take on) more credit than the nation's poorly developed economy will be able to pay in the medium term." Should Chinese development projects lag, or the exports market fail to expand, it is quite possible that China would be forced to reschedule foreign loan payments, or even cancel import contracts. Moreover, China's economic realities include an agricultural sector so backward that it employs seventy percent of the labor force and an industrial sector that is ten to thirty years out of date. Even the nation's oil potential is largely unknown in both size and quantity.

Meanwhile, despite the shock and indignation suffered by the Taiwanese as a result of America's derecognition, the industrious people of Taiwan have quickly settled down to keeping their G.N.P., which grew almost thirteen percent in 1978, and exports which shot up to thirty-six percent, galloping right along.

TABLE 10

PERCENTAGE DISTRIBUTION OF WORLD EXPORTS
BY STATUS OF DEVELOPMENT OF NATIONS

NATION'S DEVELOPMENT STATUS	Percentage Distribution of World Exports	
	1965	1975
Developed Nations	69%	67%
Developing Nations	18%	22%
Underdeveloped Nations	13%	11%
	100%	100%

SOURCE: FORTUNE Research, FORTUNE, August 1976, p. 128.

NOTE: In recent years the Developing Nations have increased their share of world trade by four percent. This increase is reflected in a two percent decrease absorbed by the Developed Nations and a two percent decrease absorbed by the Underdeveloped Nations which can ill afford it.

119

The Taiwan government, has furthermore, prudently built foreign reserves over the years. Today its seventeen million citizens sit on a comfortable seven billion dollar cushion and enjoy their capitalist status of eighth-biggest trading partner of the United States. Now Taiwan's economic planners are devising new ways to stave off competition from China. As a way to create new business K.T. Li, minister and architect of Taiwan's surging development, recommends the creation of joint ventures with American companies to produce plant-equipment in Taiwan. "Even with your devalued dollar you can't compete in selling whole factories in Asia," he says. "Your financing and engineering costs are too high. Besides, you don't know how to market in this part of the world. But in a joint venture with us, you get fifty percent." Then soft-spoken Li adds: "that's better than zero percent for both of us."[24]

Clearly competition, that mainstay of capitalism, is becoming the foundation for economic development in the Asian marketplace. Rampant inflation in the industrialized world is creating new economic opportunities for the developing nations, and governments are submitting their economies to the rigors of free enterprise to stimulate economic growth and bring their countries into the mainstream of international trade and investment. As a result a global redistribution of commodity production will occur. The more complex technologies, however, will undoubtedly remain the private preserve of the Western world for some time to come, certainly through the trying years of space colonization.

FOOTNOTES

[1]Jonathan Hughes, Industrialization and Economic History; Theses and Conjectures, (New York: McGraw-Hill Book Company, 1973), 15.

[2]Robert Moss, "Let's Look Out For No. 1!" The New York Times Magazine, May 1, 1977, 31.

[3]Rodney, Walter, How Europe Underdeveloped Africa, (Washington, D. C.: Howard University Press, 1974.

[4]D. Seers, in "The Limitations of the Special Case," Bulletin of Oxford Institute of Economics amd Statistics, May 1973, stresses the 'realism' aspect while G. Myrdal, in Economic Theory and Underdeveloped Regions, (London, 1957) stresses the 'relevance' aspect. Since African economies, as an example of underdevelopment, are integrated into the structure of the developed capitalist economies one should read the economics of J. M. Keynes in his book The General Theory of Employment, Interest and Money, (New York: Macmillan and Company, 1936).

[5]U. Hla Mynint, Economic Theory and the Underdeveloped Countries, (London: Oxford University Press, 1971), 4.

[6]Paul Bairoch, The Economic Development of the Third World Since 1900, (Berkeley: University of California Press, 1975), 201.

[7]Ibid., 202.

[8]Philip Handler, "On The State of Man," Bio Science, Vol. 25, No. 7, July 1975, 430.

[9]V.K.R.V. Rao, "Investment Income and the Multiplier In An Underdeveloped Economy," Indian Economic Review. February 1952, 48. This subject is also reviewed in W. A. Lewis' article

"Economic Development With Unlimited Supplies of Labour," The Manchester School, May 1954, 36.

[10]U. Hla Mynint, The Economics of the Developing Countries, (London: Hutchinson Publishers, 1967), 143.

[11]Pierre Jalee, The Pillage of the Third World, (New York: Monthly Review Press, 1970).

[12]Guy F. Erb and Valeriana Kallab, editors, The Developing World Speaks Out, (New York: Praeger Publishers, 1975), 86. For a clear definition of the elements of a New International Economic Order note remarks made by Mahbub UL Haq at a Conference on New Structures for Economic Interdependence co-sponsored by the Institute on Man and Science and the Aspen Institute for Humanistic Studies, the Overseas Development Council and the Charles F. Kettering Foundation held at the United Nations and at the Institute for Man and Science, Rensselaerville, New York, May 15-18, 1975. The report of that conference is titled New Structures for Economic Interdependence (Rensselaerville, New York: Institute on Man and Science, August 1975).

[13]A. Prest, Public Finance in Underdeveloped Countries, (London: Weidenfeld & Nicholson, 1962), 95. Also, read the report of the Group of Experts on the Structure of the United Nations System, A New United Nations Structure for Global Economic Cooperation, U.N. Doc. No. E/AC 62.9 (New York: United Nations, 1975), 10.

[14]Ibid., 98.

[15]Peter Berger, "Hard-Line View of Inequality Among Nations," FORTUNE, May 1977, 142.

[16]A statistical perspective of Third World economic activity may be observed in the Chapter tables.

[17]Robert moss, "Let's Look Out For No. 1!" The New York Times Magazine, May 1, 1977, 31. It should be noted, however, that the resistance by economists to Third World redistribution demands is predicated on their awareness of waste, mismanagement and inadequate planning in the developing nations.

[18]Guy F. Erb and Valeriana Kallab, editors, The Developing World Speaks Out, (New York: Praeger Publishers, 1975), 8.

[19]E. F. Schumacher, Small Is Beautiful: Economics As If People Mattered, (New York: Harper & Row Publishers, 1973), 292. Also note the observations of Ray Vicker, staff reporter of the Wall Street Journal, in his Journal article of October 14, 1977, in which he reflects on waste and mismanagement in the developing OPEC nations.

[20]This section is taken from Samuel L. Parmar, "Environment and Growth Debate in Asian Perspective," Anticipation, (World Council of Churches, Geneva), August 1973, 5.

[21]V/ M/ Dandekar, "Democratic Socialist Path to Economic Development," Mainstream," January 1974, 10-11.

[22]Harry Harding, Jr., China And The U.S.: Normalization And Beyond, (New York: China Council of the Asia Society and the Foreign Policy Association, 1979), 2-4.

[23]Ibid., 16.

[24]Roy Rowan, "Taiwan Gears Up To Go It Alone," FORTUNE, Volume 99, No. 3, 72-77.

CHAPTER VIII

SPACE INDUSTRIALIZATION: THE NEW ALTERNATIVE

"Too low they build, who build beneath
    the stars."
                    - Night Thoughts
                    Edward Young (1683-1765)

The New York Times editorialized in late
1978 that traffic jams could be expected in
space by 1985. Their writers estimated that in
less than a decade there will be at least thirty
communications satellites and half a dozen lu-
nar probes orbiting the earth. And more than
likely, space shuttles will be making regular
extraterrestrial journeys to space colonies.
These ventures certainly are not capriciously
motivated. "Rather," said astronaut Edwin A.
Aldrin in a mid-1977 Boca Raton News interview,
"the medical benefits of space exploration
alone are worth more than all the money spent
on Mercury, Gemini and Apollo." "I think," he
added, "that the space program is by far the
best bargain we've ever had." Commander Aldrin
commented further on the economic benefits of
the United States space program by pointing out
that no other American project of comparable
significance has ever been completed on time,
reasonably close to original cost estimates and
far surpassing expected results.[1]

There are many legitimate reasons for space
exploration and colonization. Put simply and
chronologically they are: (1) to orbit satellites for improved communications, celestial
transmission, weather forecasting, navigation,
resource monitoring and other purposes; (2) to
reap the by-product of space technology by -
transferring innovations and methods to many
areas of industry and medicine; (3) to compare
other planets with the earth and to study the
sun so as to better understand the earth's ori-
gin, workings and dwindling mineral reserves;
(4) to search the universe in order to learn,
among other things, whether life or even other

intelligences exist elsewhere; and (5) to create a focal point for a new intellectual renaissance that will contribute to further economic growth and still higher living standards for all people. Two decades of exploration activities have profoundly stimulated the economies of the participating nations. As a matter of fact the investment in space has an enormous payoff because it benefits a wide variety of industries. As far back as October 1965, FORTUNE writers exclaimed, consequently, that "nothing can stop this technical revolution, any more than the Mississippi River can be stopped."[2]

For centuries man has behaved as though the planet earth and its resources were infinite. Then, suddenly, in less than sixty years technological advances irrevocably altered the course of his behavior. Additionally, the Club of Rome's study of world dynamics at the Massachsetts Institute of Technology, "Limits To Growth," projected catastrophic collapse based on what is now an archaic trendline.[3] The real value of the study, then, was its revelation that raw materials must be sought in the galaxies. And so America, in 1978 embarked on a new era, one of true space travel. The age of the space shuttle (part airplane, part spacecraft) has begun thus heralding the space industrialization revolution. This marriage of technology and the marketplace is expected to improve old products, create new ones, improve all forms of communication, uncover new sources of oil, gas and minerals, expand the science of weather forecasting and set the stage for large-scale exploration of solar energy.[4]

By the end of the twentieth century the economic impact of business in space will be staggering. Generated revenues could reach thirty billion dollars and economists predict that private enterprise will capitalize more and more on the new opportunities. "As pioneering successes take place, you can expect much more of American industry to join the equivalent of a land rush into space," Paul Siegler, president of Earth/Space, Inc., a California space consulting firm, recently told Nation's Business. A major leap forward is the series of space flights planned for 1979 and 1980 beginning in the Spring of 1979 at Cape Canaveral when the first manned space shuttle, the Enterprise will fly in low earth orbit, a belt of space extending from one hundred to six hundred miles above planet earth. For the next decade the space shuttle system is expected to be fully operational, conducting experiments for industry, government and foreign interests. Since, the shuttle will accommodate four mission specialists and a sixty-five thousand pound payload, it will be a pay-as-you-go space vehicle. Whoever books space, whether private business, a United States agency or a foreign government, will pay for the cost of the mission. If there are two or more users they will split the cost. A pricing concession will be made for the European Space Agency, a ten Western European nations consortium engaged in space research, which is providing six hundred million dollars to build the Spacelab that will be flown aboard the shuttle in the 1980's. The same applies to the Canadian government which is contributing a ninety million dollar manipulator arm that will be used for launching other spacecraft from the shuttle, for repairing communications satellites, and the like.[5]

Once extraterrestrial colonization and industrialization become a fact of everyday life factories in space "can utilize the unique properties of space---weightlessness, hard vacuum, limitless energy and high vantage point---to produce large-scale benefits for all people" said George W. Jeffs, president of North American space operations for Rockwell International. Production machinery would be almost wearless and workers and equipment, without the constraints of gravity, would move about much more easily. As a result of the lower expenditure of energy individual productivity should increase. Dr. Klauss Heiss, president of Econ., Inc., of Princeton, New Jersey unequivocally echoes Mr. Jeffs view, in his prediction for the period starting about the year 2000, when he says "industrial space activities, with or without financial participation by government, will develop and sustain themselves entirely, based on the pursuit of economic interests. Once this point is reached, the space program will have become truly irreversible. Economic self-interest, again and again, has proven to be the most lasting historical motivation for human activity." "For this reason," added Mr. Siegler, "as we proceed, government more and more will have to learn to speak the language of the marketplace, or we will have to get into the private space launching business. Eventually private enterprice will compete with the National Aeronautics and Space Administration (NASA), and there will be increasing competition from abroad."[6]

However enthusiastic NASA's high-technology contractors may be many other earthling industrialists have reacted mutely to the glittering promise of the asteroids. There is, after all, the rather basic matter of costs. Even a simple experiment aboard the Enterprise will cost several hundred thousand dollars, while a small automated orbiting production plant is likely to run into tens of millions of dollars.[7] Despite these facts, Robert A. Frosch, NASA's administrator, says that his job at present is "to provide access to space and to develop basic technologies, which eventual users will need to evaluate before making investment decisions." Obviously NASA is not exactly starting from scratch. It is continually building on successful and promising experiments performed on prior space flights. Test results, mainly from those of the Skylab and Apollo-Soyuz ventures, showed that beyond the pull of earth's gravity remarkable transformations take place in materials. Crystals grow more uniformly, as much as ten times larger than on earth. Biological substances can be separated and sorted more easily, suggesting the possibility of producing purer vaccines and brand-new drugs. It has been established, furthermore, that it is technically possible to create new types of glass, various

kinds of super alloys and materials of variable
density the likes of which have never before
been seen. Some scientists already feel very
strongly that the shuttle flights are a mile-
stone for human invention comparable to the development of the vacuum pump in the seventeenth
century.[8]

It is significant, to say the least, that
the Russians and Canadians are participating in
American space experiments, that West German
and Japanese corporations are more excited about
the Shuttle than their United States counterparts, and that the European Space Agency has
enthusiastically budgeted more than twice the
NASA budget for the design and construction of
the first orbital factory in which specially-
trained space workers will manufacture alloys
in electronic furnaces. Considering all the
unknowns, perhaps the best judgment that can be
made is that while few corporations will, due
to their skepticism, care to take the plunge
into space manufacturing, none who are affected
by changes in technology can afford to ignore
the new era of innovation that is about to begin.[9] Boeing, for one, is not ignoring the
challenge. Its top management thinks that it
could run the Shuttle profitably as a commercial enterprise. Man, ever the builder, is
even planning the construction of highly-sophis-
ticated, multi-billion dollar solar-power satellites for launching before the end of the
century. Each of these would be nearly as
large as Manhattan Island and would beam energy
to earth round the clock. Approximately one
hundred of them would be expected to supply
thirty percent of United States electric power
needs. This NASA program is at the present
time too speculative for any meaningful cost-
benefit analysis. Speculative or not and however
fanciful and imaginative all of this appears
to be Lockheed has developed a folding solar
generator to provide the Shuttle with twelve
thousand watts of auxiliary power and Grumman
has designed and built a beam extruder to con-
vert flat strips of aluminum into three-dimen-
sional assemblies which will become the back-

bones of a variety of immense space structures.[10]

It is evident that the United States
government, together with industry and in cooperation with other nations, has taken specific steps toward the goal of space colonization. This dramatic effort, made possible by
the political-economic marriage of government
and business and sparked by competition, is
desirable because of the hope it offers human-
ity. A heightened sense of the limits of planet Earth, a growing awareness of its delicate
ecological balance and finite resources and its
burgeoning population attest to its need. In
America, growth has been the vehicle of rapid
and progressive change. It also has been the
source of opportunity for millions of people.
Since terrestrial resources are rapidly dwindling and the quality of life has become more
and more difficult to improve the space alternative is clearly the way to go over the long
term.

FOOTNOTES

[1]"Economic Benefits Of Our Space Program," Nation's Business, April 1978, 11.

[2]Neil R. Ruzic, "Why Are We In Space,? The American Legion Magazine, March 1979, 18-53.

[3]T. A. Heppenheimer, Colonies In Space, (New York: Warner Books, Inc., 1977), 63-68.

[4]Gerard K. O'Neill, The High Frontier: Human Colonies In Space, (New York: William Morrow and Company, Inc., 1977), 49-62.

[5]Vernon Louviere, "Space: Industry's New Frontier," Nation's Business, February 1978, 5-10.

[6]Ibid., 12.

[7]T. A. Heppenheimer, Colonies In Space, (New York: Warner Books, Inc., 1977), 91-96.

[8]Gene Bylinsky, "Industry's New Frontier In Space," FORTUNE, Volume 99, No. 2, January 29, 1979, 77.

[9]Richard D. Johnson and Charles Holbrow, editors, Space Settlements: A Design Study, (Washington, D. C.: Scientific And Technical Information Office, National Aeronautics And Space Administration, NASA SP-413, 1977), 49.

[10]Gene Bylinsky, "Space Will Be The Next Big Construction Site," FORTUNE, Volume 99, No. 4, February 26, 1979, 64-65.

CHAPTER IX

WHERETO TENDS ALL THIS?

This, then, brings us to the crux of the questions which we have addressed in enterprise analysis. We must now concentrate on the challenges of the problems; i.e., the survivability characteristics of free enterprise and its ability to serve the wants and needs of entrepreneurs, people and governments. Thus far we have dwelt at length on the past and present aspects of this question. We have assessed capitalism's strengths and weaknesses as it progressed in America from laissez-faire to partially regulated enterprise. We have, furthermore, recognized the economic justification of competition and the scope of its role in an emerging global and extraterrestrial economic system. In both Great Britain and Japan the organization of enterprise has taken on the form of a mixed economy. France is in the throes of an economic revolution. It is attempting the slowing of its inflation rate, the throttling down of its unchecked growth rate and the reversal of its long postwar drift toward state control of large sectors of the economy. The aim of the government of President Valery Giscard d'Estaing is to make the French economy competitive by minimizing intervention in business and putting an end to dirigisme, the ages-old practice of letting Paris manage almost everything. Meanwhile, in the Third World there is a concentrated effort to enter the international marketplace not only by developing an industrial economy but, as well, by demanding a redistribution of the Western World's resources as reparations for alleged colonial exploitation. Even the planned economy of totalitarian Russia is undergoing change by moving into world markets and adopting some of the trade techniques of the democratic world. In short, then, we have observed democratic laissez-faire enterprise in the Western World moving in the direction of regulated free enterprise. Conversely, totalitarian government is tending to move in the direction of a fully regulated, planned market economy.

In the early years of this century, some intellectuals in the United States were convinced that capitalism inhibited economic well-being and freedom. They believed that the hope for the future lay in greater control by government over enterprise. And, even today, there is still a tendency to regard any existing government intervention as desirable, to attribute all evils to the market, and to evaluate new proposals for government control in their ideal form. The proponents of limited government and free enterprise remain on the defensive!

Yet, it now should be clear that the difference between the actual operation of the market and its ideal operation is certainly more acceptable to conservative intellectuals than the difference between the actual effects of government intervention and their intended effects. It would seem reasonable to believe, therefore, that though the nature and form of competitive capitalism have changed, it is still the best regulator of the economy and that we only need to prohibit its violations and extend its influence.[2] Proof of this proposition is the super inflationary result of America's abused energy policies of the mid-1970's and that nation's current drift toward deregulation.

The fact of the matter is that the free enterprise economic system is far from collapse. United States capitalism and the Japanese mixed economy are proof of this. And, in Britain economic recovery is under way without recourse to authoritarian rule or a planned economy. Obviously, in the United States, other economic factors have successfully countered the self-contradictory effects of the system's tendency toward labor productivity (leading to fewer jobs) and decreased capital productivity (leading to a shortage of capital).[3] Moreover, a very wide and presumably well-qualified body of opinion, including some academic economists, nearly all businessmen, and many government officials, holds that the American economic system is the strongest in the world.

Discounting political fervor and exaggeration of free enterprise advocates, another reason for such enthusiasm is the rise, with time, in the annual output of the production system. This increased output can be relied upon to overcome the effects of the declining productivity of capital and the rising productivity of labor and to generate sufficient investment capital and jobs to maintain a stable economy. Hence, even if the productivity of capital falls it should be possible to counteract this effect simply by using more capital than before from the increased output. Likewise, even though labor productivity rises so that the number of jobs that need to be filled to achieve a given level of production declines, the total number of jobs can be maintained by overall growth in the rate of production.[4]

And, this is what seems to be happening! There is growing evidence that the economic system of the United States is being reorganized by the entrepreneurs themselves. The energy industry, and public utilities in particular, have an acute capital shortage. Unable to raise their own investment funds, some private utility companies are taking the unprecedented step of acquiring capital by charging their customers for it. The St. Louis Globe-Democrat has noted that in Missouri the Union Electric Company received approval from the Public Service Commission to charge the capital cost of constructing a nuclear power plant to its present customers (although they will receive no power from this plant, which is due to be completed in 1983, if then). Since the utilities capital is the base on which the customer's electric rates are computed, the customers will be paying the utilities a return on capital which they themselves have furnished. As a letter to the local newspaper put it, "what we have here is a case of socialism for Union Electric and private enterprise for its customers."[5] In California, utilities are asking that their customers pay the costs of options to purchase Alaskan gas when and if it becomes available in about ten years.[6] And, of course, the inclination to use public funds to guarantee private investments in synthetic fuels and other profit-motivated adventures into new energy sources is a similar maneuver. These instances are real, empirical evidence that at least in the energy sector there is a shortage of capital; that private entrepreneurs are unable to meet capital requirements out of their own earnings; and that they are not so devoted to the ideology of private capital as to reject social capital when they need it. In this sense the economic reorganization of the utilities has already begun. The question that arises is whether their expanding social economic base will be reflected in some form of public social control, so that the production and use of their power can be governed by altruistic social values such as jobs maintenance, rather than by private profit. Such profit, however, along with the assurance of unlimited growth, is their real motivation. This motivation will unquestionably falter when faced with an acceleration by organized labor in interdependent economies to extract wage and benefit gains far in excess of productivity improvements.[7]

All of this, then, tends to lead us to a determination that the life span of capitalism as it presently exists, or of its politicized successor, can be fitted into an evolutionary time frame. A radical step in that direction is now taking place. We might say that it began in 1943 when Wendell L. Willkie, American presidential aspirant, expressed a widely felt public sentiment; namely that "for years it has been recognized in the United States that if peace, economic prosperity and liberty itself were to continue in this world, the nations of the world must find a method of economic stabilization and cooperative effort."[8]

We now know that reliance solely on the laissez-faire marketplace as a panacea is not a solution to the most challenging problems of an industrial civilization. No matter how much Herbert Spencer or William Graham Sumner or Milton Friedman or Frederich von Hayek praise absolutely free enterprise as the sum and substance

136

of total freedom, one still must recognize the
need for the kind of give and take between government and entrepreneurial lobbyists that presently exists in the American democratic economic
system. Here the political economic organization
in existence is an Americanized version of Keynes' economic philosophy which contributed to
prosperity by successfully arguing that the government spend to create jobs. But even Keynes
now appears obsolete. Government priming of the
economy may put more people to work, but it cannot curb inflation to which full employment is a
major contributor. In fact creation of more public sector employment, past a certain point, can
only be detrimental to the private sector as a
whole.[10] We need only look to industrial nationalization in Keynes' Great Britain for proof
of the effects of fiscal irresponsibility.

Yet, the need for international trade makes
all nations market-oriented and some of the
staunchest supporters of laissez-faire have not
hesitated to ask the government to bail them out
of trouble.[11] It is this fact of life which, no
doubt, has brought about the current debate over
the proper response to Third World demands for a
New International Economic Order. In the politically relevant area of policy discussion two
broad positions may now be discerned. One tends
toward accommodation with Third World demands,
the other toward resistance. Both positions involve an amalgam of empirical perceptions and
moral judgements requiring decisive actions.[12]
There are those who lecture about moral obligations in atonement for the supposed crimes of
colonialism and capitalist exploitation and
those who warn of Third World revenge by the for-
mation of new cartels, the rising of raw materials prices, the reneging of debts and the expro-
priation (as in Zaire) of Western companies.

In 1965 Samuel P. Huntington published an
article entitled "Political Development and Political Decay" that attracted considerable attention in the politics of developing nations.
He warned that the rise of urbanization, literacy, communications, voting participation, mass

movements, unions and other such phenomena was leading to mass mobilization that could unleash desires governments could not satisfy. Unless these processes were slowed by improvement in the institutionalization of government, bureaucracy, and especially ruling political parties, popular restlessness would lead to instability, or political decay. "To properly institutionalize," Professor Huntington said, "governments must develop complexity and clear hierarchies in their internal organization, autonomy from the influence of various social groups, and coherence among their component parts, leading to adaptability in meeting new problems."[13] As part of this program to slow popular mobilization they must minimize competition among segments of the political elite, limit communications, and increase the complexity of the social structure.

In short, institutions existing in village society to effect mass mobilization and representation have not been recreated in today's nation states. Mechanisms to regulate conflict do exist, but are seldom if ever, backed up by commonly shared values or by the principal features of a contract: negotiations in which both sides bargain for concessions. One-party-dominant states with considerable control over popular movements have become virtually universal in developing nations. Once the centralization is established, even coups d' état, while marked by extreme hatred among elite factions and disruptions in their continuity, always return power to elites similar to those displaced. The fact that popular movements are not well-organized and are easy to keep in that position permits this continuity of power by the elites.[14]

Professor Huntington was an advisor in the United States Vietnam War effort and his article took a middle-line position on the debate about mass mobilization. It endorsed neither rule by military junta nor free elections. Instead Professor Huntington advocated a policy of détente and open discourse at the negotiating table to avoid prolonged conflict. Yet Vietnam stands virtually alone as an example of protracted civil war within a developing nation. The fact that it was so extended may have less to do with inevitable mass uprising in a world of change than with being financed and partially fought by Great Powers, containing two separate fully-formed capital cities for the same racial group, and the access of various factions to surreptitious financing from the sale of opium.[15] The biggest economic policy blunder of the Vietnam conflict was perhaps the extent to which United States and United Nations assistance freed the major patron-client network in Saigon from its dependence on the producers of goods and services. The feeding of the major network from the outside relieved it of the necessity to support itself from exports of rice and other commodities. The incentive for internal production thus gone, it becomes hard to create adequate food, comfortable neighborhoods, secure jobs, education adjusted to job availability and personal aspirations, balanced family budgets, and housing in keeping with all of these considerations. Even governments in developed nations with autonomous representative interest groups and high per capita incomes find it difficult to make adjustments which provide the above conditions for wide strata of the populace. Without such institutions and resources it becomes even more difficult; especially in circumstances of rapid social change. It is not surprising, therefore, that alienation of large percentages of the citizens of developing nations is widespread.

Poorer segments of the populace seldom translate such alienation into political activism, whether from habit, fear, or experience. They find other ways to dissipate their frustrations. Middle-class groups inclined in this direction must face the fact that it is easy for any government to break up their organizational efforts and either jail or co-opt their leaders. With this in mind it makes sense to many alienated people to give positive support to a government which offers them small reliefs from their tension, whether in the form of sports contests or a job, even while this government prevents them from making more frontal attacks on their

problems. When movements occasionally overcome
inertia to gain real, disruptive momentum, they
usually find it impossible to cope with the racial animosities which tend either to break them
apart or temporarily unite the rest of the nation
against them.[16] In this manner small elites,
composed of social and sometimes racial minori-
ties, maintain a grip on power even as alienation
increases.

Eventually, however, the need for developing
a healthy political system becomes too great for
a government to deny. Such a system in order to
survive must provide its citizens with a stable
personal environment. Developing nations once
contained such healthy political systems but
appear no longer to do so since the introduction
of extensive commerce. Today, political systems
are separate from idigenous social systems and
will remain so until the structure of international trade changes. Both developing and developed nations would like to be more independent
with social and political systems reintegrated
thus promoting their political development. This
desire is burdened, however, with a number of
concerns.

One has to do with fuel. Interdependence
requires considerable transport and sophisticated
machinery; it uses fuel. Many of the manufactured products sold in international markets use
fuel which is becoming more expensive and in
shorter supply. Obtaining it could require a
tradeoff of valuable land space, investment capital, or economic subservience to those foreign
powers who are the chief exporters. Another concern has to do with the role of multinational
corporations. These are becoming more mobile.
They have power to affect prices, demand for labor, availability of goods, and political options
in all nations; and, increasingly, they are not
based in any one nation. A third concern relates
to national defense. If a nation is dependent on
outside sources for materials needed to feed,
clothe, or shelter itself, its security is diminished. If its military machine needs outside
supplies, weapons, or fuel, it is diminished even

140

more. With the possible exception of the Soviet
Union and Canada, which have vast land and raw
material resources, the more technologically advanced a nation becomes, the greater likelihood
that this dependence will increase.

There is a basic incompatibility between
national independence and the present international system of interdependence. Multinational
corporations are interested in resources (including both material goods and human labor) that
they can combine in the easiest manner possible
and for the highest profit possible. They are
interested in resources which they can bring under organizational control and distribute themselves. A great many human, plant, animal, solar, soil, water and mineral energy resources
are physically scattered, deposited in small
quantities, and isolated from the basic communications infrastructure on which corporations depend.[17] A great many people are equally cut off
from that communications network and from money
economy. As the cost of bringing both these marginal resources and marginal markets into the
corporate economy increases, it is more profi-
table to focus on drawing profits from accessi-
ble, easily controlled resources and markets.
Urban dwellers are entirely dependent on corporate intermediaries for food, clothing, and shelter;[18] they are also compactly located for distribution purposes.

The North Atlantic nations have political
systems which are closely embedded in their
social systems and are in a position to rely on
popular support to exert some control over the
multinationals. One reason that the corporations have succeeded in gaining the independence
they have is that the people in these nations
have perceived their own welfare to be tied to
the welfare of the corporations. Should the
material welfare of these people be affected in
a manner that disturbs this perception, they can,
by controlling their own consumption, inhibit to
a degree the restrictive actions of multinational
corporations.[19]

Multinationals call for consumer democracy.
At the same time their executives join liberals
in advocating that the power to regulate be
moved into the hands of world government. Multinationals need taxes from those developed regions
to build roads, power plants, and armies in less
developed regions, such as The People's Republic
of China, so as to extract resources; if they
had to build these roads and armies themselves
they could not maintain their profits. They need
the power to manipulate tariffs and import quotas to monopolize those resources. Hence they
prefer to keep control of taxes and trade as far
from the hands of the public as possible; they
fear intervention in these matters by democratic
governments. Most of all they need markets.
They could not create adequate markets in the
developing nations without vast expenditures on
infrastructures, job training, and income spending activities. That would require heavy tax
revenues from the governments of the very nations
which supply the bulk of their present market;
those in North America, Western Europe and Japan.

Such moves might require a simplification
of lifestyle everywhere in the world since the
developing countries wish to avoid specialization of production. They do not want to be the
farmers and raw materials sources for the already industrialized nations. The recent plunge
of the People's Republic of China into the international trade maelstrom and its embrace of the
capitalist ethic are mute witness of this pos-
ture. All nations, therefore, would have to de-
vote more to growing food and developing their
own energy sources; those with food and energy
surpluses would be the only ones assured of
foreign markets.[20] Consumption habits which
wasted food or energy (whether fossil fuels or
wind or plow oxen) would be counter-productive
for national independence rather than a desirable aspect of international economic growth.
Notions of unlimited growth based on inexpensive
raw materials and expanding markets abroad would
give way to ideas of making the most of whatever
materials were available. People would need to
trade the luxury of quickly discarded consumer

products for the security of steady supplies of food, clothing, and shelter emanating from materials close to home. To do this, they might have to choose settlement patterns that abandon megalopolis for more scattered urban and rural settlements.[21]

Finally, in view of our observations in this study it seems reasonable to believe that capitalism will not vanish or collapse. Nor will it, because of its own dynamism, retain its present form. There will without doubt be degrees of changes from greater government regulation to lesser regulation, (both national and international), and back again. This phenomenon should, with time, be reflected in free enterprise and political freedom throughout the world in varying degrees and under political systems of greater or lesser authoritarian rule again in varying degrees and at different periods of time. In summary, then, an analysis of global and galactic enterprise experience of the last few years leads us to the conclusion that highly innovative multinational corporations are and will remain an important and viable factor in worldwide political economic structures and individual national development. This applies to both mother countries and host countries in which multinational companies are active. Their influence will no doubt continue into the future if they are permitted to plan their own business policy and to utilize their technical, economic and personnel possibilities. The consequences of encouraging conglomerates to establish a goal of world-wide integration may be the salvation of economic freedom and the furtherance of human rights and welfare.

FOOTNOTES

[1]Milton Friedman, Capitalism and Freedom, (Chicago: The University of Chicago Press, 1962), 197.

[2]John Kenneth Galbraith, Economics and the Public Purpose, (Boston: Houghton Mifflin Company, 1973), 234.

[3]Barry Commoner, The Poverty of Power, (New York: Alfred A. Knopf, 1976), 237.

[4]Ibid., 239.

[5]The effect of the decision by the Missouri Public Commission to allow Union Electric to recover construction costs of the nuclear power plant before the plant goes into service is described in an article in the St. Louis Globe-Democrat, January 5, 1976.

[6]For an account of the efforts by California utilities to charge their customers for options on future gas, see the Weekly Energy Report, December, 15, 1976.

[7]Robert L. Heilbroner, Business Civilization In Decline, (New York: W. W. Norton and Company, Inc., 1977), 102.

[8]Wendell L. Willkie, One World, (New York: Simon and Schuster, 1943, 199.

[9]John Kenneth Galbraith, The Age of Uncertainty, (Boston: Houghton Mifflin Company, 1977), 319.

[10]"Keynes is Dead," The Wall Street Journal, editorial, January 31, 1977, 8.

[11]John Kenneth Galbraith, The Age of Uncertainty, (Boston: Houghton Mifflin Company, 1977), 155.

[12]Peter Berger, "A Hard-Line View of Inequality Among Nations," FORTUNE, May 1977, 39.

[13]S. N. Eisenstadt, "Breakdowns of Modernization," Economic Development and Cultural Change, Vol. 12, July 1964, 349.

[14]Ibid., 351.

[15]Alfred W. McCoy, The Politics of Heroin in Southeast Asia, (New York: Harper and Row, 1972), 83.

[16]Robert E. Gamer, The Developing Nations: A Comparative Perspective, (Boston: Allyn and Bacon, Inc., 1976), 222.

[17]Ibid., 358.

[18]Richard J. Barnet and Ronald E. Muller, Global Reach: The Power of Multinational Corporations, (New York: Simon and Schuster, 1974), 158. On this subject it is interesting to note that Professor Howard Perlmutter of the Wharton School has estimated that by 1985 from 200 to 300 multinational corporations will control eighty percent of all productive assets in the non-Communist world.

[19]Ibid., 126.

[20]World Bank Mission, Nigeria: Options for Long-Term Development, (Baltimore: Johns Hopkins University Press, 1974), 129.

[21]Ibid., 130.

SELECTED BIBLIOGRAPHY

BOOKS

Abbegglen, James C. Business Strategies for
    Japan. Tokyo: Sophia University, 1970.

Adams, T.F.M.; and Kobayashi, N. The World of
    Japanese Business. Tokyo: Kodansha Inter-
    national, Ltd., 1969.

Allen, G.C. Japan's Economic Expansion. Oxford
    University Press, 1965.

Allen, R.W. Democracy and Communism: Theory and
    Action. New York: Van Nostrand Reinhold
    Company, 1967.

Al-Otaiba, Manna Saeed. OPEC and the Petroleum
    Industry. New York: John Wiley and Sons,
    Inc., 1975.

Bacon, Robert and Eltis, Walter. Britain's Eco-
    nomic Problem: Too Few Producers. New York:
    St. Martin's Press, 1976.

Bairoch, Paul. The Economic Development of the
    Third World Since 1900. Berkeley: Univer-
    sity of California Press, 1975.

Balassa, B.A. Economic Development and Integra-
    tion. Mexico: Centro de Estudios Monetar-
    ios Latinamericos, 1965.

Baldwin, G.B. Beyond Nationalisation. London:
    Oxford University Press, 1956.

Ballon, Robert J. Doing Business in Japan.
    Tokyo: Sophia University, 1968.

Balough, Thomas. The Economics of Poverty.
    London: Geo. Weidenfeld and Nicholson, 1974.

Barnds, William, editor. China And America: The
    Search For A New Relationship. New York:
    New York University Press for the Council on
    Foreign Relations, 1977.

Barnett, A. Doak. China Policy: Old Problem And
    New Challenges. Washington, D. C.: The
    Brookings Institution, 1977.

Bauer, P.T. Dissent On Development; Studies and
    Debates in Development Economics. London:
    Weidenfeld and Nicholson, 1971.

Beasley, W.G. The Modern History of Japan. New
    York: Praeger Publishing, 1970 and rev.1974.

Bell, Daniel. The Coming of Post-Industrial So-
    ciety: A Venture in Social Forecasting. New
    York: Basic Books, 1973.

Bell, Daniel. The Cultural Contradictions of
    Capitalism. New York: Basic Books, 1976.

Benedict, Ruth. The Chrysanthemum and The Sword.
    Houghton Mifflin Company, 1946.

Berliner, Joseph. The Innovation Decision in
    Soviet Industry. Cambridge: MIT Press,1976.

Bernstein, Marver H. Regulating Business By Inde-
    pendent Commission. Princeton: University
    Press, 1966.

Bradbury, Ray, et.al. Mars And The Mind Of Man.
    New York: Harper & Row, 1973.

Brady, R.A. Crisis in Britain, Plans and
    Achievements of the Labour Government. Cam-
    bridge: University Press, 1950.

Cassady, Ralph, Jr. Price Making and Price Be-
    havior in the Petroleum Indsutry. Volume 1,
    New Haven: Yale University Press, 1954.

Caves, Richard E. and Uekusa, Masu. Industrial
    Organization in Japan. Washington, D. C.:
    The Brookings Institution, 1976.

Chandler, Albert. Clash of Political Ideals: A
    Sourcebook on Democracy and the Totalitarian
    State. Third Edition. New York: Appleton-
    Century-Crofts, 1966.

Clark, J.W. Economic Regionalism and the
    Americas. New Orleans: Hauser Press, 1966.

Clecak, Peter. Crooked Paths: Reflections on
    Socialism, And The Welfare State. New York:
    Harper & Row, Publishers, 1977.

Clegg, H. Industrial Democracy and Nationalisa-
    tion. London: Blackwell, 1951.

Cocks, Paul, Daniels, Robert V., and Heer, Nancy
    W. The Dynamics of Soviet Politics. Cam-
    bridge: Harvard University Press, 1977.

Cole, Allan B.,; Totten, George O.; and Uyehara,
    Cecil H. Socialist Parties In Postwar Ja-
    pan. New Haven: Yale University Press,
    1966.

Cole, G.D.H. The Post-War Condition of Britain.
    New York: Praeger Publishers, 1957.

Commoner, Barry. The Poverty of Power. New
    York: Alfred A. Knopf, 1976.

Commoner, Barry, Booksenbaum, Howard and Corr,
    Michael, editors. Energy and Human Welfare,
    Volume II. New York: Macmillan and Company,
    1975.

Commons, John R. The Economics of Collective Ac-
    tion. New York: The Macmillan Company,
    1950.

Coombes, D.L. State Enterprise: Business or
    Politics? London: George Allen and Unwin,
    Ltd., 1971.

Cushman, Robert E. The Independent Regulating
    Commissions. New York: Oxford University
    Press, 1941, reprinted by Octagon Books,
    1972.

Cutler, Lloyd N. Global Interdependence And The
    Multinational Firm. New York: Foreign Pol-
    icy Association, Headline Series 239, 1978.

Dam, Kenneth W. Oil Resources: Who Gets What How? Chicago: University of Chicago Press, 1975.

Denison, Edward. and Chung, William K. How Japan's Economy Grew So Fast, The Sources of Postwar Expansion. Washington, D. C.: The Brookings Institution, 1976.

Destler, I.M.; Clapp, Priscilla; Sato, Hideo and Fukui, Haruhiko. Managing An Alliance: The Politics of U.S.-Japanese Relations. Washington, D. C.: The Brookings Institution, 1976.

Dimock, Marshall E. The Japanese Technocracy. New York: Walker and Weatherhill, 1968.

Ebsenstein, William. Today's Isms. Englewood Cliffs, New Jersey: Prentice-Hall, Inc., 1959.

Edwards, Sir Ronald. Nationalised Industries: A Commentary. London: Athlone Press, 1967.

Engler, Robert. The Brotherhood of Oil. Chicago: University of Chicago Press, 1976.

Eppen, Gary D. Energy: The Policy Issues. Chicago: University of Chicago Press, 1975.

Erb, Guy F. and Kallah, Valeriana, editors. Beyond Dependency: The Developing World Speaks Out. New York: Praeger Publishers, 1975.

Fairlie, Henry. The Spoiled Child of the Western World. New York: Doubleday and Company, Inc., 1976.

Fellmeth, Robert C. The Interstate Commerce Omission: The Public Interest and the ICC. New York: Grossman Publishers, 1970.

Fiorina, Morris P. Congress--Keystone of the Washington Establishment. New Haven: Yale University Press, 1977.

Fleming, John. Inflation. New York: Oxford
    University Press, 1976.

Foster, C.D. Politics, Finance and the Role of
    the Economics. London: George Allen and Un-
    win, Ltd., 1972.

Frankel, Paul H. Oil, The Facts of Life. London:
    Weidenfeld and Nicholson, 1962.

Friedenberg, Edgar Z. The Disposal of Liberty
    and Other Industrial Wastes. New York:
    Doubleday and Company, Inc., 1975.

Friedman, Milton. Capitalism and Freedom. Chi-
    cago: University of Chicago Press, 1976.

Friedman, Milton. Money and Economic Develop-
    ment. New York: Frederic A. Praeger, Inc.,
    1973.

Friedrich, Carl J. Totalitarian. Cambridge:
    Harvard University Press, 1954.

Galbraith, John Kenneth. A Contemporary Guide
    to Economics, Peace and Laughter. Boston:
    Houghton Mifflin Comapny, 1971.

Galbraith, John Kenneth. Economics and The Pub-
    lic Purpose. Boston: Houghton Mifflin Com-
    pany, 1973.

Galbraith, John Kenneth. The Affluent Society.
    Boston: Houghton Mifflin Company, 1969.

Gamer, Robert E. The Developing Nations: An Eco-
    nomic Perspective. Boston: Allyn and Bacon,
    Inc., 1976.

Gasset, Jose Ortega Y. The Revolt of the Masses.
    New York: W.W. Norton and Company, 1932.

Greaves, H.R.G. Democratic Participation and
    Public Enterprise. London: Athlone Press,
    1964.

151

Greenberg, Edward S. Serving the Few, Corporate Capitalism and the Bias of Government Policy. New York: John Wiley & Sons, Inc., 1974.

Griffin, Clare E. Enterprise in a Free Society. Chicago: Richard D. Irwin, Inc., 1949.

Haberler, Gottfried. Stagflation: An Analysis Of Its Causes And Cures. Washington, D. C.: American Enterprise Institute, Reprint No. 64, March 1977.

Haberler, Gottfried. Oil, Inflation, Recession and The International Monetary System. Washington, D. C.: American Enterprise Institute, Reprint No. 45, June 1976.

Hammond, Allen H., Metz, William D. and Haugh, Thomas H., II. Energy and The Future. Boston: American Association for the Advancement of Science, 1973.

Hanson, A.H. Nationalisation, A Book of Readings. London: George Allen and Unwin, Ltd., 1963.

Hanson, A.H. Parliament and Public Ownership. London: Cassell, 1961.

Hanson, A.H. Public Enterprise and Economic Development. London: Routledge Publishing, 1959.

Harding, Harry, Jr. China And The U.S.: Normalization And Beyond. New York: Foreign Policy Association, Inc. for the China Council of the Asia Society, 1979.

Harrington, Michael. The Twilight of Capitalism. New York: Simon and Schuster, 1976.

Hartshorn, J.E. Oil Companies and Governments. London: Faber and Faber, 1966.

Heilbroner, Robert L. The Future As History. New York: Harper and Row, Publishers, 1959.

Heilbroner, Robert L. Business Civilization in Decline. New York: W.W. Norton and Co., Inc., 1976.

Heilbroner, Robert L. Inquiry Into The Human Prospect. New York: W.W. Norton and Co., Inc., 1974.

Henry, John M., editor. Free Enterprise: An Imperative. Wichita, Kansas: Herbert Hoover Presidential Library Association, 1975.

Heppenheimer, T.A. Colonies In Space. New York: Warner Books, Inc., 1977.

Hewins, Ralph. The Japanese Miracle Men. London: Oxford University Press, 1967.

Hicks, J. The Crisis of Keynesian Economics. London: Oxford University Press, 1974.

Hirschmeir, Johannes and Yui Tsumehiko. The Development of Japanese Business, 1600-1973. Cambridge, Massachusetts: Harvard University Press, 1975.

Hla, Mynint, U. The Economics of the Developing Countries. London: Hutchinson and Company, Ltd., 1973.

Holzman, Franklyn. International Trade Under Communism. New York: Basic Books, 1976.

Hughes, Johnathan. Industrialization and Economic History: Theses and Conjectures. New York: McGraw-Hill Book Company, 1973.

Hunt, R.N. Carew. The Theory and Practice of Communism. Harmondsworth, England: Penguin Books, Ltd., 1963.

Jalée, Pierre. The Pillage of the Third World. New York: Monthly Review Press, 1970.

Kahnert, K. Economic Integration Among Developed Countries. Paris: Organization for Economic Cooperation and Development, 1969.

Kase, Francis J. People's Democracy: A Contri-
    bution to the Study of the Communist Theory
    of State and Revolution. Leyden: A.W.
    Sijthoff, 1968.

Kash, Don. E., Devine, Michael D. and Others.
    The Role of Research, Development and Demon-
    stration in Reaching a National Consensus on
    Energy Supply. Norman: University of Okla-
    homa Press, 1976.

Kelf-Cohen, R. British Nationalisation 1945-
    1973. London: Macmillan St. Martin's Press,
    1973.

Kelf-Cohen, R. Twenty Years of Nationalisation.
    London: Macmillan St. Martin's Press, 1969.

Keynes, J.M. The General Theory of Employment,
    Interest and Money. New York: Macmillan and
    Company, 1936.

Kolb, Albert. East Asia. London: Methuen and
    and Company, Ltd., 1971.

Landis, James. The Administrative Process. Cam-
    bridge: Harvard University Press, 1938.

Lekachman, Robert. Economists At Bay. New York:
    McGraw-Hill Book Company, 1976.

Lequiller, Jean. Japanese History of the Twen-
    tieth Century, Le Japon. Paris: Editions
    Sirly, 1966.

Levinson, Charles. Capital, Inflation And The
    Multinationals. New York: The Macmillan
    Company, 1971.

Little, I.M.D. A Critique of Welfare Economics.
    Oxford: Clarendon Press, 1957.

McKinnon, Ronald I. Money and Capital in Econo-
    mic Development. Washington, D. C.: Brook-
    ings Institution, 1973.

Mathias, F.J. Economic Integration in Latin
America. Austin, Texas: Bureau of Business
Research, University of Texas, 1969.

Melady, Thomas P. Western Policy and the Third
World. New York: Hawthorn Books, 1967.

Mitchell, Edward J., editor. Perspectives on
U.S. Energy Policy: A Critique on Regulation. New York: Praeger Special Studies,
1976.

Moley, Raymond. Daniel O'Connell, Nationalism
Without Violence, An Essay. New York: Ford-
ham University Press, 1974.

Morley, James. Dilemmas of Growth in Prewar Japan. Princeton: Princeton University Press,
1974.

Moore, W.S. Regulatory Reform Highlights. Washington, D. C.: American Enterprise Institute
for Public Policy Research, 1976.

Morgenthau, Hans J., editor. Trade And The Dollar: Coping With Interdependence. New York:
Foreign Policy Association, Headline Series
242, 1978.

Morrison, H. Government and Parliament. London:
Oxford University Press, 1954.

Moynihan, Daniel Patrick. Maximum Feasible Mis-
understanding. New York: The Free Press,
1969.

Myrdal, G. Economic Theory and Underdeveloped
Regions. London: Oxford University Press,
1957.

Neibuhr, R. Relfections On Democracy As An Al-
ternative to Communism; Can The 'Free
World' Hope For The Evolution of Democracy
In Any--Even Some Of the Newer and Poorer
Nations? New York: Columbis University
Forum, Summer, 1961.

155

Normanton, E.L. Accountability and Audit of
    Governments. Manchester: Manchester Uni-
    versity Press, 1966.

Ohkawa, Kazushi and Rovosky, Henry. Japanese
    Economic Growth. Stanford, California:
    Stanford University Press, 1973.

Patrick, Hugh and Rovosky, Henry. Asia's New
    Giant: How The Japanese Economy Works. Wash-
    ington, D. C.: The Brookings Institution,
    1976.

Phillips, A., editor. Promoting Competition In
    Regulated Markets. Washington, D. C.: The
    Brookings Institution, 1975.

Plamenatz, John. Ideology. New York: Praeger
    Publishers, 1970.

Posner, M. Fuel Policy. New York: The Macmillan
    Company, 1973.

Prest, A.R. Public Finance In Underdeveloped
    Countries. London: Weidenfeld and Nichol-
    son, 1962.

Prest, A.R. Public Sector Economics. Manchest-
    er University Press, 1968.

Prior, Frederic L. Property and Industrial Or-
    ganization in Communist and Capitalist Na-
    tions. Indiana University Press, 1973.

Pryke, R. Public Enterprise in Practice; The
    British Experience of Nationalisation Over
    Two Decades. London: MacGibbon & Kee,
    1971.

Raphael, Jesse S. Government Regulation of Busi-
    ness. New York: The Free Press, 1966.

Reid, G.L. and Allen, K. Nationalised Indus-
    tries. London: Penguin Books, 1970

Revel, Jean Francois.The Totalitarian Tempta-
    tion. New York: Doubleday, 1977.

Robens, Lord. Ten Year Stint. London: Cassell, 1972.

Robson, P. Economic Integration in Africa. London: Allen and Unwin, 1968.

Robson, W.A. Nationalised Industry and Public Ownership. London: George Allen and Unwin, Ltd., 1960.

Rodney, Walter. How Europe Underdeveloped Africa. Washington, D. C.: Howard University Press, 1974.

Rubin, Jerry. Do It!: Scenarios of the Revolution. New York: Oxford University Press, 1976.

Rustow, Dankwart A. and Mugno, John F. OPEC: Success and Profits. New York: New York University, 1976.

Samuelson, Paul. Economics. New York: McGraw-Hill Book Company, 1967.

Schlesinger, Arthur M., Jr., The Decline of Greatness. Boston: Houghton Mifflin Company, 1962.

Schumacher, E.F. Small Is Beautiful: Economics As If People Mattered. New York: Harper & Row Publishers, 1973.

Schumpeter, Joseph. History of Economic Analysis. New York: Oxford University Press, 1954.

Schwartz, Bernard. The Economic Regulation of Business and Industry, A Legislative History of U.S. Regulatory Agencies. 5 volumes. New York: Chelsea House Publishers, 1973.

Scitovsky, Tibor. The Joyless Economy. New York: Oxford University Press, 1976.

Seed. Allan H.. III. Inflation: Its Impact On Financial Reporting And Decision Making. New York: Financial Executive Research Foundation, 1978.

Selekman, Sylvia Koplad and Selekman, Benjamin M. Power and Morality in a Business Society. New York: McGraw-Hill Book Company, Inc., 1956.

Shepherd, W.G. Economic Performance Under Public Ownership. Cambridge: Yale University Press, 1965.

Smith, B.L.R. and Hague, D.C. The Dilemma of Accountability in Modern Government. New York: The Macmillan Company, 1971.

Smith, Hedrick. The Russians. New York: Ballantine Books, 1976.

Spitz, David. Democracy and the Challenge of Power. New York: Columbia University Press, 1958.

Spitz, David. Patterns of Anti-Democratic Thoughts. New York: The Macmillan Company, 1949.

Stone, P.B. Japan Surges Ahead, The Story of An Economic Miracle. New York: Frederick A. Praeger, Publishers, 1969.

Stromberg, Roland N. After Everything, Western Intellectual History. New York: St. Martin's Press, 1975.

Taylor, George W. Government Regulation of Industrial Relations. New York: Prentice-Hall, Inc., 1948.

Thirlwall, A.P. Growth and Development, With Special Reference To Developing Economies. Cambridge, Massachusetts, Schenkman Publishing Company, 1972.

158

Thornhill, W. The Nationalised Industries, An
    Introduction. London: Nelson, 1968.

Tivey, L.J. Nationalised Industries Since 1960.
    London: George Allen and Unwin, Ltd., 1973.

Tocqueville, Alexis de. Democracy in America
    1835-39). ed. Phillips Bradley. New York:
    Alfred A. Knopf, 1956.

Toynbee, Arnold. Civilization on Trial and The
    World and the West. New York: New American
    Library, 1976.

Trani, Eugene P. Treaty of Portsmouth, 1905.
    Lexington, Kentucky: University of Kentucky
    Press, 1969.

Tucker, Robert W. The Inequality of Nations.
    New York: Basic Books, 1977.

Tugendhat, Christopher. Oil: The Biggest Busi-
    ness. New York: C.P. Putman's Sons, 1968.

Turvey, R. Economic Analysis and Public Enter-
    prise. London: George Allen and Unwin,
    Ltd., 1972.

Turvey, R. Public Enterprise. London: Penguin
    Books, 1968.

Ulam, Adam B. Philosophical Foundations of Eng-
    lish Socialism. Cambridge: Harvard Univer-
    sity Press, 1951.

Ul Haq, Mahbub. The Poverty Curtain: Choices
    For The Third World. New York: Columbia
    University Press, 1976.

Veblen, Thorstein. The Theory of Business Enter-
    prise. New York: The New American Library
    of World Literature, Inc., 1958.

Von Mises, Ludwig. Planning For Freedom. South
    Holland, Illinois: Libertarian Press, 1962.

Walder, David. The Short Victorious War. New York: Harper and Row, 1974.

Weidenbaum, M.L. Government Mandated Price Increases: A Neglected Aspect Of Inflation. Washington, D. C.: American Enterprise Institute, 1975.

White, John A. Diplomacy of the Russo-Japanese War. Princeton, New Jersey: Princeton University Press, 1964.

Wilson, F.M.G. Administrators in Action. London: George Allen and Unwin, Ltd., 1961.

Yanowich, Murray, compiler. Contemporary Soviet Economics: A Collection of Readings from Soviet Sources, 2 volumes. New York: International Arts and Sciences Press, 1969.

Yoshino, M.Y. Marketing In Japan. Los Angeles: University of California, 1975.

NEWSPAPERS AND MAGAZINES

Alvarez, A. "Beyond All This Fiddle," Times Literary Supplement, March 1968.

"Bank of Japan Cuts Loan Fee 1/2 Point, to 6%," The Wall Street Journal, March 14, 1977.

Berger, Peter. "A Hard-line View of Inequality Among Nations." FORTUNE, May 1977, pp. 139-142.

Breckenfeld, Gurney. "Governments' Hammerlock on Business." Saturday Review, July 10, 1976.

Burck, G. "Transportation's Troubled Abundance." FORTUNE, July 1971, p. 88.

"Burns Says It's Time For Oil-Rich Nations to Become 'Bankers' For Poor Countries," The Wall Street Journal, March 11, 1977.

Bylinski, Gene. "Industry's New Frontier In Space." FORTUNE, Volume 99, No. 2, January 29, 1979, pp. 77-84.

Bylinski, Gene. "Space Will Be The Next Big Construction Site." FORTUNE, Volume 99, No. 4, February 26, 1979, pp. 63-68.

Duberman, Martin. "The Agony of the American Left." New York Times Book Review, March 23, 1969.

Glass, George. "The Changing Dimensions of Government-Company Relations." Middle East Economic Survey, 17 May 1968, p. 26.

Hershman, Arlene. "Regulating the Regulators," Dun's Review, January 1977, pp. 34-36.

"High Hurdles for Imports." TIME, March 14,1977, pp. 46-47.

Janssen, Richard F. "Economic Shock Wave from Oil-Price Rises in '73 Still Hurts West." The Wall Street Journal, March 10, 1977.

"Japan's Foreign Trade--The Perils of Success." The American Banker, November 15, 1976.

Jordan, Robert Paul. "Siberia's Empire Road, The Riber Ob." National Geographic, February 1976, pp. 145-181.

"Keynes Is Dead," The Wall Street Journal, editorial, January 31, 1977 and Reader Responses, February 17, 1977.

Kirk, Donald. "The High Cost of Doing Business With Japan," Saturday Review, March 19, 1977, p. 21.

Kraar, Louis. "Adversity Is Helping the Japanese Refashion Their Future," FORTUNE, October 1976, pp. 126-132.

Louviere, Vernon. "Space Industry's New Frontier," Nation's Business, February 1978, pp. 25-38.

"Marketing in Japan Takes Twisty Turns, Foreign Firms Find," The Wall Street Journal, March 9, 1977.

Meyer, Herbert E. "This Communist International Has a Capitalist Accent," FORTUNE, February, 1977.

Morgens, Howard J. "A Third Century Look at the Balance Between Government and Business," Nation's Business, October 1976.

Moss, Robert. "Let's Look Out For No.1!" The New York Times Magazine, May 1, 1977.

"Oil Buyers Beginning to Cut Purchases from OPEC States Raising Prices 10%." The Wall Street Journal, January 6, 1977.

"Oil Consuming Countries to Draw Closer," The Oil and Gas Journal, July 24, 1972.

Percy, Charles H., Senator. "A Prescription For Curing Our Regulatory Ills," Nation's Business, December 1976.

Rice, Donald. "Shortages and Economic Planning." The Wall Street Journal, March 14, 1977.

Rose, Sanford. "Third World 'Commodity Power' Is A Costly Illusion." FORTUNE, November 1976.

"Russia's Trouble With Reforms." TIME, January 26, 1970.

"Schlesinger's Czardom Takes Shape." TIME, March 7, 1977.

"Slower Economic Growth Raises Risks of Protectionism." The Wall Street Journal, December 26, 1976.

Solberg, Carl. "The Tyranny of Oil." American Heritage, December 1976.

"Soviets Wink At Doctrine, Flirt With Profits." Steel, September 16, 1968.

"Swallowing a Bitter Tonic." Time Magazine, December 13, 1976.

"The Battle of the Barrels Begins." TIME, January 3, 1977.

"Two-Tier Oil Pricing Hasn't Weakenes OPEC, Western Energy Group Aide Says." The Wall Street Journal, December 22, 1976.

Vicker, Ray. "Petrodollar Leak." The Wall Street Journal, October 14, 1977.

Vicker, Ray. "Push for Petroleum." The Wall Street Journal, March 8, 1977.

"World Energy: Decisions That Must Be Taken Soon." Financial Times, August 3, 1973.

PROFESSIONAL JOURNALS

Abel, Lionel. "Beyond The Fringe." Partisan Review, 80, (Spring 1963):111.

Adams, James Luther. "The Evil That Good Men Do." Voices of Liberalism, 2, (1942): 48.

Akhminov, H. "Market Socialism Embarasses Soviet Ideologists," Institute for the Study of the USSR Bulletin, (June 1968): 106.

Akins, James E. "The Oil Crisis: This Time The Wolf Is Here." Foreign Affairs, 51, (April 1973): 475.

Barraclough, Geoffrey. "The Great World Crisis I." New York Review of Books, (January 23, 1977): 61.

Baumol, William. "Smith v. Marx on Business Morality and the Social Interest." The American Economist, (Fall 1976): 41.

Bottomley, A. "Keynesian Monetary Theory and The Developing Countries." Indian Economic Journal, (April-June, 1965): 70.

Boyd, James Weinberg, Alvin M. and Meadows, Dennis L. "Resources and Economic Growth, The American Future: A Dialogue." The Wilson Quarterly, 1, (Autumn 1976): 56.

Chenery, Hollis B. "Restructuring The World Economy." Foreign Affairs, 53, (January 1975): 254.

Chiaramonte, Nicola. "The Will To Question." Encounter, (November 1953): 1-2.

"Consider Japan." The Economist, London, (1963): 23.

Correy, Lewis. "Problems of Peace. IV: The Middle Class." Antioch Review, 5, (Spring 1945): 87.

Dandekar, V.M. "Democratic Socialist Path to Economic Development." Mainstream, (January 1974): 35.

Goldman, M.I. "The Soviet Economy In The 1970's." Current History, 55 (October 1969): 288.

Hall, Peter. "Going American?" New Society, 18, (July 15, 1972): 117.

Handler, Philip. "On The State of Man." Bio Science, 25, (July 1975): 430.

Hasan, Parvez. "The Investment Multiplier in an Underdeveloped Economy." Economic Digest, 3, (1960): 59.

Heckscher, August. "The Fair Deal." The Reporter, 1, (April 26, 1949): 18.

Johnson, Chalmers. "The New Thrust in China's
   Foreign Policy." Foreign Affairs, (Fall
   1978): 125-37.

Kagawa, Toyohiko. "The Social and Economic Outlook in Japan Today." Journal of the Royal
   Central Asian Society, 37, (1950): 124-131.

Landreth, H. "Creeping Capitalism in the Soviet
   Union?" Harvard Business Review, (September 1967): 134-140.

Liberman, E.G. "Role of Profits In The Industrial Incentive System of the USSR." International Labor Review, (January 1968:
   91-96.

McCloskey, Herbert. "The Fallacy of the Absolute Majority Rule," Journal of Politics,
   11, (1949): 67.

Mannes, Marya. "Penalties of Prosperity." The
   Listener, 64, (December 1, 1960): 62.

Parmar, Samuel L. "The Environment and Growth
   Debate in Asian Perspective," Anticipation,
   World Council of Churches, Geneva, (August
   1973): 15.

Reischauer, Edwin O. "The Postwar 'Miracle'."
   The Wilson Quarterly, 1, (Summer 1977): 56.

Rifkin, Jeremy. "The Red, White and Blue LEFT."
   The Progressive, 35, (November 1971):14-21.

Robson, W.A. "Problems Of Industrial Nationalisation." Political Quarterly, (January 1969).

Sakamoto, J. "Industrial Development and Integration of Underdeveloped Countries."
   Journal of Common Market Studies, (June
   1969): 19.

Shanahan, Eileen, moderator. "Regulatory Reform: A Survey of Proposals in the 94th
Congress." A Round Table Discussion published by Washington, D. C.: American En-
rerprise Institute for Public Policy Research, 1976.

Solomon, Richard N. "Thinking Through the China
Problem." Foreign Affairs, (January 1978):
324-56.

Spencer, Daniel L. "An External Military Presence, Technological Transfer and Structural
Change." Kyklos, 18, (1965): facs. 3.

Stewart, Richard. "The Reformation of American
Administrative Law." Harvard Law Review,
(June 1975): 56.

Woodward, C. Vann. "The Future of the Past."
American Historical Review, 85, (February
1970): 718-722.

OTHER PUBLICATIONS

Al-Mahdi, Muhammad S. "The Pricing of Crude Oil
in the International Market: A Search for
Equitable Criteria." A paper presented at
the Eighth Arab Petroleum Congress, Algiers,
May-June, 1972.

Ashby, Eric. "Investment in Man." Presidential
Address to the British Association for the
Advancement of Science, August 28, 1963.

Gaitskell, H.T.N. Socialism and Nationalization.
London: Fabian Tract 300, 1956.

Safer, Morley and Friedman, Milton. "Will There
Always Be an England?" New York, CBS News
60 Minutes Broadcast Transcript, Volume 9,
November 28, 1976.

Schroeder, G.E. "Soviet Economic Reforms: A
Study in Contradictions." Soviet Studies,
July 1968.

Spulber, Nicholas. "Is The USSR Going Capitalist?" Key Factors in Economic Growth. Ann Arbor: University of Michigan Bureau of Business Research, 1968.

"Third World Special Task Force." Proposals For A New International Economic Order, Mexico City, August 21-24, 1975.

PUBLIC DOCUMENTS

American Bar Association Reports, 41/368.

Federal Trade Commission, The International Petroleum Cartel. Washington, D. C. U.S. Government Printing Office, 1952.

Gaishi-kei Kigyo. "Kansuru Chosa-hokoku-sho Report on Companies With Foreign Capital)," Ministry of Trade and Industry, September 20, 1968.

Great Britain. Parliament. Parliamentary Papers, 1944, Cmnd. 6527, "White Paper on Employment Policy."

Great Britain. Parliament. Parliamentary Papers, 1944, Cmnd. 6610, "Report of Technical Advisory Committee on Coal Mining (Reid Report)."

Great Britain. Parliament. Parliamentary Papers, 1945, Cmnd. 6669, "Report of Committee of Inquiry Into the Gas Industry (Heyworth Report)."

Great Britain. Parliament. Parliamentary Papers, 1956, Cmnd. 9672, "Report of Committee of Inquiry Into the Electricity Supply Industry (Herbert Report)."

Great Britain. Parliament. Parliamentary Papers, "Reports from select Committee on Nationalised Industries, Oct. 1952 and July 1953."

(Report and Accounts):
1956/7/304 (Scottish Electricity Board).
1957/8/187 (National Coal Board).
1958/9/213 (Air Corporations).
Special Report 1958/9/276.
1959/60/254 (British Railways).
1960/1/280 (Gas Industry).
1962/3/226 (Electricity Industry).
1963/4/240 (B.O.A.C.).
1964/5/313 (London Transport).
1965/6/77 (Gas, Electricity and Coal Industries).
1966/7/340 (Post Office).
1967/8/371 (Ministerial Control of Nationalised Industries) 3 vols.
1967/8/298 Special Report; the Committee's Order of Reference.
1970/71/514 Relations with the Public.

Great Britain. Parliament. Parliamentary Papers, 1957, Cmnd. 262, "Report on Purchasing of the British Transport Commission."

Great Britain. Parliament. Parliamentary Papers, 1969, "Labour Government's Economic Record."

Great Britain. Parliament. Parliamentary Papers, March 2, 1960. "The Coal Board's Guillebaud Report.

Great Britain. Parliament. Parliamentary Papers, 1957, "Labour Party Policy Pamphlet No. 1", British Transport, n.d., Industry and Society.

Great Britain. Parliament. Parliamentary Papers, 1969, Cmnd. 4027, "Reply by Government on Ministerial Control of Nationalised Industries."

Great Britain. Parliament. Parliamentary Papers, 1968, Cmnd. 3561, Price and Income Board, "Proposals for Bus and Railway Fare Increase in London."

168

Great Britain. Parliament. Parliamentary Papers, 1958, Cmnd. 585, "Exchange of Correspondence between Minister of Transport and Chairman of British Transport Commission."

Great Britain. Parliament. Parliamentary Papers, 1960, Cmnd. 1203, "Public Investment in Great Britain."

Great Britain. Parliament. Parliamentary Papers, 1961, Cmnd. 1337, "The Financial and Economic Obligations of the Nationalised Industries."

Great Britain. Parliament. Parliamentary Papers, "Annual White Papers on Government Financing of the Nationalised Industries capital requirements. Stated in 1961 as 'Government Expenditures below its line;' then became "Loans from the Consolidated Fund;" from 1968, with the establishment of the National Loans Fund, became "Loans from the National Loans Fund."

Great Britain. Parliament. Parliamentary Papers, 1967, Cmnd. 3437, "Nationalised Industries: A Review of Economic and Financial Objectives."

Kaplan, Eugene J. Japan: The Government-Business Relationship, A Guide For The American Businessman. U.S. Department of Commerce, February 1972.

Khatkhate, D.R. "Analytic Basis of the Working Monetary Policy in less Developed Countries," International Monetary Fund Staff Papers, November 1972.

Otauka, Kasuhiko. "Balanced Industrial Structure and Transfer of Technology: A Study of Technology Transfer in Small-Scale Industries," Ministry of International Trade and Industry, 1972.

"Office of Communications v. Federal Communications Commission," 359 F. 2d 994, 1003-04, D. C. Circular, 1966.

"Possibility of Intelligent Life Elsewhere In The Universe," Report prepared for the Committee on Science and Technology, U.S. House of Representatives, Ninety Fifth Congress, First Session, by the Science Policy Research Division, Congressional Research Service, Library of Congress, October 1977.

"Space Manufacturing Facilities (Space Colonies)," Proceedings of the Princeton/AIAA/NASA Conference of May 1974 and May 1975 published for the National Aeronautics and Space Administration by the American Institute of Aeronautics and Astronautics, Inc., New York, March 1, 1977.

"Space Settlements, A Design Study," NASA SP-413, edited by Richard D. Johnson, NASA Ames Research Center and Charles Holbrow, Colgate University for the Scientific and Technical Information Office, National Aeronautics and Space Administration, 1977.

U.N.C.T.A.D. "Towards a Global Strategy for Development." Report by the Secretary-General of the United Nations. Conference on Trade and Development, Document TD 3, Rev.1, United Nations, New York, 1968.

U.S. Congress, Senate. "Interstate Commerce Act, S. Doc.1093, 49th Congress, 2d Session, February 4, 1887.

INDEX

INDEX

imports (cont.) 67,68,
  69,70,72,73,94,113,
  142
individualism 24,87
Industrial Development
  Executive 35
Industrial Expansion
  Act 32
Industrial Reorganization
  Corporation 32,34,36
inflation 18,31,36,39,41,
  57,61,72,73,75,78,104,
  106,107,108,120,133,137
Inosemtsev, Nicolai 17
Institute of World Economy
  and International Rela-
  tions 17
interdependence 16,141
International Monetary
  Fund 41
Interstate Commerce Com-
  mission 47,48,49,52,
  54,55
investment 4,39,40,41,49,
  56,69,72,73,75,104,107,
  108,109,110,120,125,128,
  135,136,140
Izvestia 18

J

Jaffe, Louis 55
Jeffs, George W. 127

K

Keynes, J.M. 24,40,104,
  136,137
Kosygin, Alexei 17
Krupp Industries 16

L

labor 4,10,11,12,34,
  49,52,63,75,78,118,
  134,135,136,141
Laborites 23
Labor Party 31
Landis, James 48
leasing
  equipment 13
  outer continental
  shelf 61
Lequiller, Jean 84
Li, K.T. 120
Liberal Democrats 83,
  96
Liberals 41,142
Liberman, E.G. 10,14
liberty 3,51,136
licensing 49,52
Lipsky, Seth 118
loans 29,32,41,87,97,
  118
Lockheed Corporation
  35,95,96,129

M

Macmillan, Harold 30
market 95,120,134,
  141
  American 93
  black 18
  conditions 63
  domestic 67,96
  export 19
  fair 52,69
  foreign 67,142
  free 53,69,78,103,
  107,108
  gray 18
  home 31
  international 96,
  140

174

INDEX

S

Sakharov, Andrei 14
satellites 125,127,129
Schumpeter, Joseph 3
Schroeder, G.E. 12
Secretary of Agriculture
  50
sector
  agriculture 106,118
  capitalistic 42
  consumer products 17
  energy 136
  export 17,18
  industrial(ization)40,
  42,105,114,118
  large 133
  manufacturing 106
  private 23,24,26,27,
  29,30,31,33,34,36,42,
  137
  public 23,26,27,29,33,
  34,35,36,41,42,93,137
  top priority 17
  trade 19,88
Securities and Exchange
  Commission 49,52
Selekman, Benjamin M. 2
Selekman, Sylvia Koplad 2
shareholders 13,31,88
Shaw, George Bernard 27
Sherman Act 54
Shipbuilding and Indus-
  try Act 33
Siegler, Paul 126
Skylab 128
Smith, Alfred E. 54
Socialism 9,10,11,36,135
society 58,69,83,86,97,
  103,138
Spacelab 127
Special Drawing Rights 75
Spencer, Daniel L. 84
Spencer, Herbert 136
stagflation 61,73

Stalin, Josef 10
steel, 25,34,69,83
Stone Age 16
Sumner, William
  Graham 136
supply and demand
  law of 9,17
system 57
  banking 87,107
  competitive 47,48
  economic 5,73,83,
  97,133,134,135,137
  free enterprise 56,
  58,83
  government 50
  industrial 2
  international 141
  monetary 73,75
  political 83,93,96,
  140,141,143
  pricing 68,69,70
  production 135
  quota 65
  regulatory 53
  social 140,141
  space shuttle 127
  state 24
  transportation 55
  United Nations 108

T

Tanaka, Kakuli
  Prime Minister 96
tax (es) 142
  highway 63
  hire purchase 27
  investment (credit)
  40
  laws 72
  policies 78
  purchase 26,27
  sales 41